The Franklin River Springs To Life

A Memoir
Doug Sockhill

First published 2025
Copyright © Doug Sockhill, 2025

Doug reserves the right to be identified as the author of this book in accordance with the copyright act, designs and patents act 1988. This book is a memoir detailing events that have happened in Doug's life according to his memory at the time. Names and characters may have been changed to preserve the dignity of people mentioned in the story.

Publishing Consultant - Just Sparkle Books
Editor - Ann Nearchou
Book Cover design and layout – Melanie Raevn Brasch

Purchase of copies and further information about the author and his adventures can be found by scanning the QR code on the back cover or following this link:
https://linktr.ee/dougsockhill
This QR code also gives you access to the book's Facebook page for more photos and updates.

Cover photo. The epitome of exhaustion. Myself, Deb, Rob, Angela, and Rob.

ISBN: 9780645919035

Foreword

Doug Sockhill has led a very wild life – and when things weren't wild enough, it was Doug who always seemed to be the one "cranking up the volume".

When Doug told me he was writing an autobiography, I figured it would be about the size of four Peter Fitzsimon's novels because Doug has packed so much into life (and continues to do so). I also felt a little nervous.

Having had a pre-read of Doug's autobiography, I can attest that the adventures related are faithfully told, though some selective memory might be sneaking in here and there!

Doug's choice of using his adventure rafting down the changing nature of the Franklin River as a metaphor for his life seems appropriate because rivers typically zig-zag to follow fault lines. My experience in having been a mate of Doug's for over 40 years is that Doug was normally the one causing the fault lines to appear! Also, when you are down in a river, much of the surrounding landscape is invisible to you – and so it is with Doug's recounting of tellable stories within a sea of less-tellable ones.

This book is a thoroughly enjoyable read, it brings back fond memories of the escapades I was involved in and fleshes out other adventures I was only vaguely aware of. May the adventures continue.

Enjoy.

Peter Tait

Dedication

To my amazing wife, Ann, who has stood by me despite the churning rapids and has skilfully enticed me away from the ethical edge into a more respectful lifestyle.

Contents

Index of Terminologies	8
PROLOGUE	11
PART ONE: The Early Years	15
Chapter 1 Setting one's personality: before life starts....	16
Chapter 2 The Start	19
Chapter 3 School days, early days	28
Chapter 4 First Big Rapids	34
Chapter 5 University Life	37
Chapter 6 The Bike	42
PART TWO: The Turbulent Years, Crazy Days	47
Chapter 7 The rapids are rising…Fun times in the Burdekin…	48
Chapter 8 The Thunder Rush portage	54
Chapter 9 The Great Ravine	56
Chapter 10 Jail Time	62
Chapter 11 Disaster! - bubble, bubble, toil and trouble	68
Chapter 12 Travel	72
Chapter 13 Cyprus	90

Chapter 14 Reflections at lunch and work experiences   95

Chapter 15 Yachting days (from what I can remember)   109

Chapter 16 The wedding and the week of honeymoon mayhem.   123

Chapter 17 The end of the rapids??? Brazil, September 2023   130

Chapter 18 Pakistan October 2024   133

**PART THREE: Still Waters Run Deep:
The Franklin Changes the Nation**   141

Chapter 19 Still Waters   142

Chapter 20 The Franklin River springs to life, and changes the nation.   144

Chapter 21 The Later Years   147

References   153

Appendix 1: Snapshots in Time (Editor's cuts)   154

i. Getting high   154

ii. Shark attack   155

iii. Beach getaways   155

iv. OUCH What the fuck was that???   156

v. Hello, is the Queen available?   158

vi. Anyone for chocolate crackle cake?   158

vii. Mount Garnet adventures: the wild west experience	160
viii. Cooktown re-enactment ceremony police encounter	162
ix. Petrie Terrace watch house (now called The Barracks)	162
x. Two train events	163
xi. Venice	165
xii. Welcome to East Germany - one year after the wall comes down	165
xiii. 28 hours in Santiago airport	166
xiv. A day in the life of a sugar mill production manager	168
xv. Enjoying retirement???	170

Appendix 2: Notes from Burdekin Hash House Harriers (BH^3) circa 1980's 172

Acknowledgements 180

Index of Terminologies

Ambrose golf competition Where (normally 4) golfers play in one team and use the best positioned ball location for each subsequent shot.

Bacon angle The angle of cooking bacon at which the bacon fat automatically runs off the BBQ plate. Normally determined after your yacht runs aground.

Cal Neva hotel and casino A famous casino on the border of California and Nevada that was partly owned by Frank Sinatra when he was in the Rat Pack. It was rumoured the Mafia were silent part owners.

Crushing A term used in sugar mills to define when a factory is operational. Refers to the cane being crushed between rollers to extract the cane juice.

Down Down A compulsory fast drink awarded at a Hash meeting, when you do something stupid, or not.

Frank Sinatra's Rat Pack A group of four celebrities who performed in the late 1940's through to the 1960's. Led by Frank Sinatra.

Hash or Hash House Harriers Not what you are thinking, no drugs involved, only moderate amounts of alcohol. It is an international running club as well.

Junk A fishing boat, typically made of wood, often used by potentially illegal immigrants to venture towards Australia. Its method of construction intrinsically provides for successful demolition by burning when its useful life has expired.

Kick turn A snow skiing term where you flick from side to side in an attempt to slow your speed down the mountain that is too steep to ski gently.

Maslow's hierarchy of needs Abraham Maslow was an American psychologist who wrote a paper in 1943 titled 'A theory of human motivation'.

Maslow's hierarchy of needs - Wikipedia

OPC Optimum piss content, or optimum blood alcohol content. This is a term used to describe when you are most likely to play your best golf (without uncontrollably falling over).

Portaging If a rapid is too dangerous, one has to unpack everything and walk or climb around the rapids.

Rapids These are formed when strong water flows over rocks in a river. They can be dangerous.

Reel to reel tape recorder A recording device that precedes mobile phones. Typically used in court houses.

Roping a rapid If possible, instead of portaging, guide the rafts down the edge of a rapid using ropes tied to each end of the raft.

SAF Sustainable aviation fuel is made from vegetative matter and can be used interchangeably with jet fuel. It is an emerging product.

Spinnaker A large sail used at the front of yachts when the breeze is following from behind.

Stopper Water flowing over a rock or log can form strong undercurrents that can trap a rafter under water, stopping them from leaving the area and potentially leading to drowning.

The big house Slang for a jail. A good place to stay away from.

The Go-Go's If you don't know who the Go-go's are I genuinely feel sorry for you. Look for, 'We Got the Beat' on Spotify.

Toxic management style A destructive management style mostly used by narcissists and psychopaths for their own unfair advantage.

Turbo-pissing A competition where the winner is one who can reach the longest distance whilst urinating. Usually a male dominated sport.

Verballing Slang (of the police) to falsely implicate (someone) in a crime by quoting alleged admission of guilt in court.

Prologue

We are halfway through our rafting trip down the Franklin River in the wild untamed jungle that defines southwest Tasmania. There are six of us, each in our own raft. In the rafts we have waterproof barrels containing all our food, clothes, camping gear and rafting equipment.

We have been immersed in so many different aspects of this now famous river. From its early life as a small, fragile bubbling mountain stream, growing to thunderous rapids, and mesmerising deep still waters with their magical cliff reflections.

Each night we stop and set up camp on the side of the river. This is a time for pondering and reflection.

I am developing the viewpoint that the Franklin River, from its birth high in the Tasmanian mountains, and its journey to the Indian ocean off western Tasmania, is emblematic, a metaphor for life, perhaps, for my life.

A river's character is formed by the terrain through which it flows. Its behaviour could be influenced by events such as the proposed dam that would, forever, change the river's flow and indeed, its natural beauty.

A person's personality may be influenced by the disposition of their parents. A person's behaviour is often influenced by life's events. It is likely to change as we mature. A premise is developing in my mind, gaining strength like the river we are on.

A person's life starts off so small and fragile. We grow into our more turbulent years through our midlife. Then we emerge into a wiser, quieter person. For many of us this is the deep-thinking and relatively quiet phase of our lives, formed with some wisdom. I am identifying different stages of my life, events in my life as I encounter the different characteristics of the Franklin River.

I can just see the lead rafters in the distance through the rising mist, as they make it successfully through the turbulent rapids and pull off to the side. They are giving us the thumbs up, but it doesn't look convincing, they look like drowned rats. It's cold. The water from high in the mountains has melted from snow. My breath turns to vapour. I can feel the moisture in the air.

I go through the training instructions in my mind. I must use the current, and not fight it. I must lean back and avoid large stoppers. I must avoid submerged trees. If I fall in, I must position my feet downstream and look for the grab rope. There is too much information, and I know there will be no time to think if I capsize. I don't have time to contemplate the incredible scenery all around us. I remember one of my life mottos that always challenges me. 'What can possibly go wrong?'. Yeah right!

Here I go, it's my turn, and I feel somewhat petrified. With an almost overpowering feeling of trepidation, I ease myself into the raft and push off into the fast-flowing current. I pull the straps tight on my life jacket and helmet. I wedge my feet into the raft's side walls hard so I can lean right back and get leverage with the paddles in the water. We are in single person rafts. I can't rely on anyone else. It's me only. I have no rafting experience. I start paddling, hard. The stopper (a standing wave that traps the raft) is right in front of me. The size is much larger than I gauged from the bank. Down I go, into the valley of water. The experience is scary and exhilarating at the same time. I feel myself losing control. Water erupts in my face as I get flung overboard when the raft flips over.

Water and bubbles gurgle all around me, the shock of the cold water takes my breath away. My mind instantly questions me, did I have time to take a breath before I fell in? I can't remember....

The Franklin River starts its life high up in the central highlands near Lake Saint Clair. It meanders through these mountains as a small stream forming Lake Undine and Lake Hermione as it progresses. The first easy glimpse of the river is from the Lyell Highway which stretches west to east across central Tasmania. From there the Franklin winds its way around the mountain named Frenchman's Cap. This mountain range consists of large steep terrain. It is a bold landscape. This develops the river's character as it twists and turns through these grand canyons. Over centuries the river has relentlessly cut its way through the mountain valleys, dominating everything in its path; slowly but surely gouging deeper and deeper into the mountainous terrain. This creates the tremendous rapids, the cliffs, the stone sculptures, the chasms, the deep still water basins with the awe-inspiring terrain that defines the beauty of this world heritage wilderness area.

This unique valley was threatened in the 1980's when the Tasmanian government pushed strongly to dam the mighty river. A protest movement grew from a small group of Tasmanian conservationists to an Australia-wide revolt which changed the political landscape of the country. The Franklin came to life and asserted its influence. It won the battle for the preservation of its natural beauty.

Rafting the Franklin is a huge logistical undertaking. Less than 500 people per year get to experience this amazing adventure, a sign that it is not a straightforward pursuit. One should take at least 12 days of food in case floods hold up progress. If all goes perfectly well, it takes about a week on the water. Don't bet your last dollar on 'that horse coming in'! Water levels can rise very quickly after rain, which occurs frequently on the west coast. This quickly makes the rapids unpassable, so you must just wait, and wait. Once you start down the river, there is no easy turning back. Total commitment.

In November 2024 (at the time of writing this book), a person became pinned by his leg in rocks. He was walking through the edge of the rapids, scouting the river for the way forward. He slipped and his foot became lodged in the rocks. He was waist deep in water. He spent all night in the river as attempts were made unsuccessfully to free him. In the end his leg had to be amputated to get him out alive. The operation was performed under the water. He was taken by helicopter to hospital in a critical condition.

Mum's family - Uncle Bill Maguire, Ma - Margaret (Manny) Maguire, Pa - Jack (Tibby) Maguire, Mum - Betty Maguire Sockhill, and Uncle Jack Maguire.

PART ONE
The Early Years

Chapter 1

Setting one's personality: before life starts....

I often reflect that I would not be here but for one word my grandfather (Mum's father) uttered, "Medic".

John Maguire, or Pa as we knew him was in World War 1, fighting in the trenches in Bullecourt, France. He never talked to me about the war. I was too young to think of asking. When I visited the war museum in Canberra, they had a display showing the trench warfare in Bullecourt, and information describing the situation. I must say it didn't look like a nice place to be. Pa took some shrapnel in the leg that pierced his artery. He started to bleed profusely but had the presence of mind to yell out loud over the noise of the bombing, for a medic, whilst trying to put pressure on the wound himself. Help arrived just in time, but he ended up losing the leg. It was a close call.

Pa was an amazing person. Having one leg was no obstacle. With Ma's (Margaret) help, he took his family on several 5-week long camping trips to remote locations. Everything they needed was packed into one car: tent, food for 5 weeks, cooking equipment, clothes, 3 kids and one dog. He built two houses with one leg. He walked along the beaches for hours, surf fishing, with one leg. Even in his 70's I remember him walking up and down steps with one leg. I don't think Pa even saw having one leg as a disability. I think Pa's zest for life shone through brightly in my Mum.

Dad - Brian Sockhill at work. Shell Lab 1951, age 22

My Mum, Bet Sockhill nee Maguire, was very active and liked exploring. She went to New Zealand in her 20's and took a working holiday for 12 months. Not many single ladies took that sort of risk back in the 1940s. She left a stable job and a serious relationship to do so. Apparently, on leaving, she said to her boyfriend, Brian, 'I'm off on a holiday for 12 months. If you're still around when I get back, maybe we could get back together and work something out'. Glad they did; that's why I'm here. I am their third child.

Mum and Dad travelled a lot; in Australia, and around the world. They mostly did tours that involved bushwalking in amazing areas, from Chile to Europe. Even in late middle age, they still went on specialised international walking tours. They were always active and always seeking new adventures.

Mum was very fit and athletically gifted. She played netball at state rep level.

I never met Dad's parents. His father was in charge of the Bundaberg post office, so I can only imagine he was an organised person.

Dad was more conservative than Mum, but also very fit. He was a foundation member of the Northcliffe Surf Lifesavers Club on the Gold Coast. The surf club and accommodation consisted of tents on the beach. He was a scientist working at Shell in Melbourne. That's where he met Mum. She was the secretary. Dad was more the deep thinker, working with the facts.

So, I started off with a mixture of 'genes' - some risky, some deep thinking, a conflicting mixture, perhaps.

As we go through life, we have experiences that build on our personality and define our character. Experiences that help establish and build our appetite for risk.

Chapter 2

The Start

So how does a river start, what determines its personality and character? I haven't been to the start of the Franklin, but I recall a bushwalking trip in NSW that describes my thoughts on this, my thoughts on how a river starts. We were walking high up in the NSW mountains, where there are no rivers.

In the distance we can see the Kosciuszko Mountain tops. We have been walking for three days. When we started, we were walking through trees and along beside small bubbling creeks. We are now above the treeline, and there are just shrubs and grasslands. The birds are chirping, and a soft breeze is working with the sweat to cool me down. We are on a five day through walk, and we have brought everything, except water. The river will provide that. My sister and my girlfriend (Ann) are with me. I thought it would be a good challenge for Ann as she doesn't really like bushwalking, and I want to find out how much she likes me and how much tolerance she has for risky pursuits.

It's late afternoon and we are about two hours out from the log cabin that would provide us very basic shelter for the night. We are walking through the valleys. We can hear a storm starting in the distance, echoing around the mountains. We quicken our pace, as we hear the storm intensifying, getting closer. We have heavy packs and can't move fast enough. Ann is struggling with the weight of her backpack. We know where we must get to, but we are losing the battle to beat the storm. We see the threatening black clouds rolling up the valley, a strong wind pushing them faster towards us. Before long the thunder is cracking, near deafening, demanding our attention. We are powered by adrenaline.

Ann is petrified of lightning; I didn't realise how much. She thinks we are going to die. She is now yelling at me and I'm not sure why – is it so I can hear over the noise of the thunder or because she is mad at me? I suspect both. 'What the hell are we doing out here?? This is crazy - when's it going to stop??' I am not sure if she is enquiring about the storm, or the walk, or our relationship and am not game to ask for clarification! 'Shit Doug, I'm scared we're gunna get struck!' she yells fearfully as the sky puts on its fireworks show.

The rain starts. My sister and I grab Ann's pack to share between us so we can make better time. We are walking through steep mountain valleys, so it is difficult to see the approaching storm clouds. When we turn the corner below a spur in the hills we see the hut in the distance. This is our protection from the lightning. The rain starts pelting down and the lightning ricochets off the trees on the hill tops around us. Frantically we push on, the rain stinging our faces. Finally we make it to the safety of the hut, feeling like drowned rats but very relieved.

My girlfriend is NOT happy!

A couple of days later we are running out of water and need to go exploring to find more. It occurs to me we may be too high up to find a river. Eventually, between two ridges, we find a large clump of grass, from which a trickle of water emerges, left over from the storm perhaps. So small it takes a while to fill our water bottles. But it is nice and clean.

THIS is the start of a river.

The landscape is defining the river's initial character. Fragile and pure, just like a new-born child. I didn't realise at the time, but where we found that water was most probably one of the streams feeding the mighty Murray River. Who could have predicted that such a small trickle of water would combine with other water sources and grow to become an iconic water course, over 1000 kilometres long!

(We finished the walk without any further major issues. Ann stayed with me, and we have been married since 1989.)

I digress - back to the Franklin and how I came to be rafting it.

I was working in the sugar industry in North Queensland in 1984, living in the country town of Ayr. When people asked me where I live, I normally said Townsville, because no one knew much about Ayr.

It was the middle of summer when I received a phone call. The heat haze was alive. It was everywhere, shimmering off the roads, the grass, the buildings. It was suffocating. Just standing still in the shade was enough to have you break into a sweat.

'Hi Doug, we're rafting down the Franklin very soon and someone has had to pull out due to illness. If you are keen to come you need to decide now. We all need our own raft. You'll need to purchase all your rafting equipment and be in Melbourne next fortnight. You'll need a very good sleeping bag, wet suit, and warm waterproof clothes. Are you interested?'

What my friend was describing was so far removed from my reality. You couldn't even buy a good sleeping bag in Ayr! It was a big call at the time to go rafting at the other end of the country. Flying in 1984 was expensive and buying all the rafting equipment would add up.

'Tell me more, what are the rapids like?' I query with trepidation. I have heard stories of people getting caught in 'stoppers' whilst rafting and drowning, never to be seen again.

'Well, we trek around the worst of them, if they're too big.', my friend says reassuringly.

'OK, I'm in', I hear myself replying, with a tone which hides my anxiety.

I had never been rafting before, and if I knew how strenuous it would be, I probably would have declined. But I was in the high energy phase of my life, keen to explore and take chances, living on the edge.

What could possibly go wrong, right? The rapids were beckoning.

Before long I arrived in Hobart and went to the house where the others were busy preparing for this trip of a lifetime. They were busy. The large lounge floor was completely covered with everything we needed; food, camping equipment, bottles, bags, ropes, more ropes, sleeping bags, rafts, repair gear, tents, cameras, books etc. etc. I was astounded at the extent of equipment and food. All this food had to be put inside plastic bags inside waterproof barrels and everything had to fit inside our rafts. What seemed like chaos eventually morphed into a workable plan.

The next day we took off early for the three-hour road trip to where the Collingwood River crosses the Lyell highway. This is the normal starting location as the Collingwood merges with the Franklin soon after. Everything was removed from the cars and the rafts pumped up and stacked high with all the equipment and food. Everything was securely tied in so it would (hopefully) not get lost if we capsized, when we capsized.

At this location the river is deceptively calm and shallow, very non-threatening. The river is a bubbling brook, the water barely 150mm high above the rounded rocky riverbed. Beautiful trees reach down to the water's edge, casting a tranquil shade pattern over the stream. Where the sun shone through it reflected off the water in a sparkling array of light. Above the sound of the burbling water, you could hear the birds chirping. The setting invites you in. It is compelling. It is relaxing. It is deceptive.

There was very little signage back in 1984 to mark the potential threats downstream. The police were in the area advising people not to raft the river. Maybe they were concerned about the dam protests further downstream as well as for the safety of people. We pressed on despite their encouragement not to. I revisited this site in 2024 and I was astounded by all the signage at the starting point. One of the signs reads......

WARNING

This is NOT the place to learn white water skills.

This river system is dangerous.
Several people have died travelling on it.

You will be exposed to risks that include:

REMOTENESS removed from immediate aid and assistance

RUGGEDNESS the surrounding terrain is rough, making travel difficult

RAIN river levels may rise ten metres or more, even during summer

RAPIDS grades 1 – 6 exist on this river

Whitewater hazards to be faced include undercuts, stoppers, strainers, logs, boils and holes.
If you don't know how to identify and overcome these hazards

DON'T ATTEMPT THIS TRIP.

Factors involved in the death of people on the river include:

ENTRAPMENT

INEXPERIENCE

ENTANGLEMENT

EQUIPMENT FAILURE

OVERCONFIDENCE

FLOODING

There were photos on the sign depicting rafters floating upside down in the raging waters. The rafts were not visible below the water. Neither were their heads. Just their legs were sticking up out of the water.

Another sign attempts to absolve the State of Tasmania of any responsibility should you get injured or die on the river.

Another explains all the equipment you should have with you and don't dare leave without it. There are sign-in registers etc. etc. Yet another sign explains correct river conduct even saying don't forget to take your shit out with you... bla, bla, bla.

I wonder if signs like these had been installed back when we started, would I have done a U-turn on the spot and hitched back to Hobart? I wonder what most people would have done.

What could possibly go wrong?

It is six kilometres to the point where the Franklin merges with the Collingwood. It is still a small stream at this point and quite often we found ourselves having to pull the rafts over the shallows. Not an easy task on the wobbly slimy rocks. A twisted ankle would not be welcome at this stage of the adventure. Not at any stage in fact.

At day's end we find a relatively flat area to camp for the night, under the canopy of the rainforest. Camping on the Franklin is next level amazing. The constant background sound of the river, the total rainforest aspect, green everywhere, the stars at night, twinkling so bright they appear to bounce around and look alive.

It is not too wet, so we start a campfire to complete the magic. 'How good is this place?', I start to verbalise my thoughts as we sit around the fire. 'This is just fantastic, the whole experience. The soothing noise from the bubbling creek, the beauty of the forest, the complete setting of the mountains in the background. I am so lucky to get invited on this adventure. I can't thank you guys enough.' We continue to yarn about the trip so far, to marvel at the logistics it has taken to get to here. 'How long have you been preparing for this trip?' I ask. The answer confirms my suspicions. They have been preparing for months. First the literature search to analyse how difficult it is. Then the research to determine what equipment is best to use, kayaks or rafts, what size of raft, what safety equipment is required etc. Then planning out the food, up to ten or twelve days for six people, and obviously everything needs to be packed properly to be waterproof. Then going out and buying everything.

'What do you know about the rapids later on in the trip?' I venture not sure if I want to know the answer. One of the guys explains, 'The river gets stronger as we travel down. There are many side streams and waterfalls that add to the flow along the way. We have very detailed maps showing the rapids and a guidebook that explains how to manage them. If they are too dangerous, we don't go down, and we must "walk" around them.'

I am not sure whether to feel excited, scared or comfortably relaxed and content. Will I be able to handle the rapids? Will I let the team down? What happens if I capsize? Will everything get wet? Will we lose some of the precious possessions? Will I get swept downstream with no one to pick me up? I wonder how much sleep I will be able to get at night if it is raining and everything is cold and wet?

I look around and try to gauge the mood of our group of intrepid travellers. It is the first time on this river for all of us. At least they have rafted other rivers. Not me. The two guys who came up with the idea of this trip seem confident. They have completed so much prep work. They seem to know what is going on. They appear organised. However, I have no experience to ground my thoughts. I sense anxiety in the group. I feel tension as I introduce the more detailed questions. Some of the answers follow a telling pause. Am I getting the whole story in the answers to my questions?

I am so tired that sleep smothers my thoughts. Not even the cold can keep me awake.

I hear the birds chirping. It must be early in the morning. People are moving around outside my tent. My brain slowly gets into gear, and finally I remember where I am. The recollection of last night's campfire beside the river eases back to my consciousness. I emerge from my comatose state. Luckily, I had bought a very high-quality feather down sleeping bag. It has managed to partly shield me from the intense cold, which I can feel on my exposed face. I emerge from the tent and take in the surroundings again. I am refreshed by how nice this setting is. The problem is however, that I must now get into my cold damp wetsuit that had no chance of drying overnight. The sooner I do this, the sooner I can start to warm up with my body heat.

This daily ritual proves to be the biggest challenge of the trip. Tougher than consciously heading into the giant rapids in my one-person raft. Tougher than portaging up and over the cliffs.

We set off paddling fast in a futile attempt to warm our aching bodies. About mid-morning we see a single raft up ahead in the distance, parked on the side of the river, with only one person in it. We are gobsmacked. Who would attempt this feat alone, this is definitely a team adventure. Having backup for when you capsize or get injured is a fundamental part of the survival plan. If there is an emergency, we have no communication with reality, wherever that is, whatever that means.

We reach the lone person, still aghast, and start a cautious conversation. Then, a total conundrum dawns on us. He asks us if he can join our crew. He had intentionally rafted down the first day and a half and parked up waiting for someone to come along and tag onto. He is too far down-river to backtrack to the highway. He gambled on rafters coming along and having no real option but to let him join.

This puts us in a real predicament. I wonder how prepared this guy is? How much food does he have? What are his rafting skills? How agile and strong is he? And these are the less serious thoughts entering our minds. For example, what do we do if he injures himself on the trip? Even the most coordinated and fit person can get seriously injured, and evacuating anyone is a major undertaking. There are very few walk-out tracks, and they are very arduous walking, even for a fit, uninjured person. If there is an issue, we will probably have to abandon all our equipment and walk out.

We have an impromptu team meeting in private, and I express my thoughts. 'This guy must have been waiting for a group to come along. I wonder how capable and prepared he is? Can we just leave him here, surely another group will come along before too long?' A discussion ensues and we somewhat reluctantly decide to let him join. I am really in two minds. While it turns out not to be a bad decision, he has very little food, which is an issue because you burn a lot of energy on a trip like this, with all the vigorous exercise. His lunch consists of half a handful of nuts and sultanas, while we tuck into a large carbs diet to stay sustained. The worry is that over several days fatigue may set in without adequate sustenance. We feel it in our own best interest to give him some food to help avoid this situation.

We continue our journey, and the water slowly gets deeper as side streams join in. These consist of wonderful vibrant waterfalls, cascading and bouncing over the rocks, sparkling in the sunshine, sending rainbows in all directions. The rafting becomes easier as the river gets deeper. There is less sliding the rafts over the rocks and more paddling. The river is gaining strength as it continues. It is vibrant and alive at this early stage in its development. I reflect on my own life at this point in time.

Chapter 3

School days, early days

My first brush with the law started early in life, I was so young I can't quite remember my age, but probably about ten. I was caught stealing lollies up town in Sarina (North Queensland), where I grew up as a child. The cafe owner knew Mum and rang her up to deliver the news. When she got off the phone we knew we were in big trouble, we could see it in her eyes. Mum knew the local police and (I suspect with some pre-arrangement) organised a visit for us. They were very informative, having an animated discussion with us and showing us inside the cells (with the door shut), and then saying, 'This is where the bad people spend the night'. It was a scary experience for a ten year old. Lesson received, but unfortunately the learnings weren't enduring.

I must admit to being a pyromaniac. Again, I made an early start. My friend (who shall remain anonymous; let's call him Brad) and I were about ten years old. We were at Campwin beach near Sarina in the August school holidays. We had what seemed like a great idea at the time, to light a small fire at the bottom of the headland, just for fun. This being prior to my Chemical Engineering learnings I didn't understand that fire races uphill. The headland covered about 2 hectares and was covered in long dry grass. A row of houses stood on top of the headland, one of which we were renting for the holidays. To our shocked surprise, the flames rose ferociously and raced up the hill. We tried valiantly to put the bush fire out with a bucket of water, but it was in vain. We watched helplessly as the flames rushed up the hill towards the row of houses. The feeling of dread swept through me uncontrollably. Luckily there was a mowed section of grass between the high grass and the houses, which acted as a firebreak and saved the day. When the fire stopped at the 'fire break' there was great relief. Dad was furious when he found out what had happened. We could have set the houses alight and he let us know it.

My most memorable day at primary school was in grade 3 when, on reflection, I think I reached peak academic performance. I was the only kid who knew the answer to, 'What is 9 divided by 2?' No-one else had a clue. A big moment in time which may have defined my career in engineering!

My next big moment came in grade 7 when I got heatstroke from stoking the wood fired clay kiln all day in the hot sun. It was my proud responsibility to cook all the clay sculptures that were made in art class. I remember hallucinating badly that night and my parents calling the doctor for help. I can still clearly remember the hallucination, it is vivid in my mind to this day; Dad was walking across Niagara Falls on a tightrope. And then the ceiling fans started leaving the ceiling and came crashing into me as I lay on the lounge room floor. Ouch.

As young kids we received 5 cents per week pocket money for doing chores. Not a lot of money, so my brother and I went on strike. No more chores done till we received a pay rise. Dad was too busy at work to notice, but Mum doubled down. She went on strike too and stopped cooking for us. So, we started eating Vegemite sandwiches 3 times a day, because that was the extent of our cooking prowess. A couple of days in, Dad noticed what was happening and asked, 'What's with all the Vegemite sandwiches?'. We told Dad about the strike action. Now Dad was a sugar mill Manager and knew all about strike action and how to handle it. His quick reply beamed out, 'This strike is now officially over!'. That was the end of that. It was quite a while before we got an increase in pay. Little did I know at the time that I would have many more involvements with strike action during my own career in the sugar mills. It's a good thing I started practising early in life.

(In hindsight I now realise why my parents were so frugal. They were young during the depression years. Their parents would have struggled during these years, which impacted my parents.)

Weekends were spent racing sailing dinghies at Mackay. These were great days and set up my love for sailing and yachting for life. I suspect it also created a sense for adventure and risk taking, as sailing outside of Mackay harbour in a small dinghy at the age of seven was a fairly unusual endeavour. I remember feeling a real sense of adventure, and loving it, as we ventured out through the harbour heads.

Another major plus from sailing was winning soft drinks. Our sabot dinghy was called Coca-Cola. We were sponsored by Coca-Cola. Whenever we won, we received a carton of Coke. This was a big deal at the time. Prior to this we very rarely enjoyed the pleasures of soft drinks. Soft drink was too expensive, apparently. Our 5c per week pocket money didn't stretch that far either.

At Sarina High School I was simply just a big nuisance. I did three years at Sarina State High then 2 years at Churchie in Brisbane (Church of England Grammar School (top shelf stuff, apparently)). We were booked in since the day we were born to attend as boarders.

At the end of grade nine Dad sat me down and we had a father to son discussion. He told me it was time to start taking things more seriously at school. He was genuinely concerned with my lack of commitment; was it really that obvious? Fortunately, I listened.

My most memorable highlight at Sarina High was the day my maths teacher sent me to the headmaster's office with a long note describing how bad I was and what I had done to disrupt the class. She told me to give the headmaster this note when I went to his office. She had had enough, and this was the last straw. It was very unusual for a student to get sent to the headmaster's office, and I was thinking it wasn't going to end well. I was shitting myself.

Potential disaster spurns creativity. The headmaster's office was clearly visible from our classroom as it was right across the parade ground, so I couldn't not go into the office. The teacher would be checking in on me. As I entered the office I was preparing my hands for the worst. (THE CANE was still in use in 1974.) This was going to hurt. Then I had a brain wave, risky, but it may work. The headmaster made me sit in the side office for quite a while to make me sweat. When I finally received the audience, I casually said to the headmaster; 'Sir my maths teacher wants to know if there is a formal parade tomorrow morning as she needs to prepare for it, if it's on'. I kept the note hidden deep in my pocket. The headmaster bought the ruse, and I avoided the sore hands. Off I went back to the classroom and threw the note in the bin on the way through. A good day at the office!! Lesson: take your chances!

I think one of the lessons I have learnt through life is that what you get out of it depends on what you put into it. An example of this was learning German in grades 8, 9 and 10. I started off failing German, not interested at all. Then the classes started to also take in some of the cultural aspects of the country, and this aroused my interest. I started putting in and soon my grades went from fail to 80%, from bottom of the class to near top. I was enjoying learning with a more holistic approach. Not just the language, but about life in Germany and how people related to each other.

At Churchie there was less opportunity for nuisance behaviour. The teachers were generally more in control, more inspiring and there was a healthier academic competition. I often wonder what would have happened to me career-wise if I had stayed in Sarina? Not a happy ponderance.

I was a boarder at Churchie. We were allowed to go into the city on Saturday nights. A couple of us went in and managed to get into a hotel bar, I guess the checks weren't as thorough in those days. So, we went into the bar for a beer and the first person I saw was my chemistry teacher. Oh crap, what now, this will get back to school for sure. My teacher called me over, and we tentatively approached, shaking in our shoes. Unbelievably he shouted us a beer, and said, 'You didn't see me in here, ever, right?' We're like yeah, no problem, but we were completely mystified. Later we came to realise we were in a gay bar, and he didn't want that to get back to Churchie either. (Back in the 70's homosexuality was largely unacceptable and even illegal)

Lesson: Take your chances!

On another visit into the city, a co-boarder and I were approached by people representing a happy clapper group. We were suckered into going into their church and lining up with the other newbies. I don't know how this works, but everyone in the line was falling over backwards when touched lightly on the forehead by the 'priest'. I was not a believer and was wondering what would happen to me when it was my turn. I still don't understand this, but I too fell over backwards on the touch. I can only assume one gets swept up in the emotion of it all. Luckily, I could smell trouble here and never went back. They prey on the vulnerable.

Unfortunately boarding at Churchie was toxic. It was either bully or be bullied. It was a good place to escape from, but it did give me a good education and set me up for an engineering degree.

Instead of going to "schoolies week" myself and two school friends caught a train to Young in central NSW and took jobs fruit picking. We camped on the farm along with the other fruit pickers. This proved to be a great experience, meeting amazing people from all walks of life. Some of them were really tuff nuts, working hard by day and playing very hard by the campfire each night. We learned from their life stories, about what to do, and equally what not to do.

We moved on to Griffith to work for Yates, tending to lettuce in great long paddocks. It was very hot work, over 40 degrees C, working all day in the sun. Griffith was going through an interesting time. Don McKay (a local reporter) had been murdered 5 months earlier, shot down in a hotel car park. The rumours of Griffith being a drug capital were rife, and Don McKay was exposing the villains. We befriended some locals who took us on a tour of the "grass castles". These are mansions that are allegedly built from drug money.

Whilst having a pub meal, we were approached and asked if we wanted a night job. This got our attention as it was so hot working during the day. The offer became more intriguing as our new friend ventured, 'Whatever you earn in 5 days working for Yates, we can offer you in one night. Just one thing though, to get to the work location, we'll drive you, but we need to blind fold you for the drive. No problems, it's all safe. Are you interested?'.

Aaaaah, let me think about that,......umm... 'NO THANKS,' I replied politely. I often think back to that point of time in my life and wonder what would have happened if I had agreed to go! Would I have escaped from that potentially captive environment??

I had learned that some chances are best left undone! Too close to the edge!

(I later came to realise, through TV documentaries and news articles, that the Griffith drug cartels had moved in from the cane fields of North Queensland, allegedly. More on this later.)

Also, on reflection, I am so glad I just didn't take the schoolies week option. It is so shallow. I look back at the experience I gained from this working holiday as being quite formative in my development. Mixing with such a range of personalities whilst camping on the farms was an insightful experience on my own river journey of life. It taught me about the importance of using initiative and developing relationships, which would become very important in my working career and life in general.

These experiences were character building just like the side streams enter a river and make it stronger and develop the river's strength and temperament.

I continued my river journey and the rapids started rising.

Chapter 4

First Big Rapids

I wake in the middle of the night. I can hear the rain pounding onto my flimsy tent roof. I wonder how much we have had, especially upstream. I'm feeling nervous. We know the river can rise quickly, and then fall just as fast. We are about a day upriver from the start of the Great Ravine. I know that a higher level makes the rapids in the ravine unpassable. I have trouble sleeping, wondering what this rain means to our progress. We have tied the rafts up high so we are confident they will remain above the rising water.

At first light we go to the river to check on the rafts and continue measuring the water level rise. I can feel the extra flow in the river compared to yesterday. The rapids look stronger, they are louder. After breakfast we recheck the level.

We have a big decision to make. People have died rafting this river. (Prior to 2010 the river had taken at least nine lives; two at Big Fall, two at Pig Trough, two at Cauldron, and one each in Trojans, Coruscades and Descension Gorge. In the summer of 1984/85 twenty-two people were airlifted out of the river.). The water level is high but steady. It is a difficult judgement call to make. We don't want to wait around unnecessarily because we could get held up again further downstream. Our food supplies won't last indefinitely.

Late in the morning we reluctantly decide to push off. Take the risk!

We have read the guide map and know to expect our first rapids very soon. We anxiously approach each bend and strain our ears, hoping to hear them first so we can prepare. Our plan is to pull over prior to the rapid and try to get a look over it from the shoreline so we can plot the best way through. Anticipation rises with each bend. We are not sure what to expect. We pass waterfalls tumbling down from the side canyons, adding to the water flow. They are spectacular in their own right, with the sun bouncing off the falling water droplets. The river is gaining strength. The riverbanks are now steeper, and the water flow is picking up speed, becoming more turbulent. We can feel the change in the force of the water. The river's personality is changing with the increase in flow and the steepness of the river banks. We are on high alert.

We hear it together, faint at first, and increasing quickly as we round the bend. We pull over to the side and tie up the rafts. Working our way along the riverbank and up the side we get a good view of the rapids and discuss the best pathway forward. I am trying to memorise this, as I know when I'm in the rapids I won't have much time to think. I have done a lot of surf skiing on my paddle board in rough ocean waves and feel confident. I have good balance and reasonable strength but know I mustn't be complacent. I have been told the rapids can be deceptively powerful.

The plan hatched; we return to the rafts. The more experienced rafters go first to test our plan and hopefully survive so they can pick up anyone who subsequently capsizes.

It's my turn. I dig my feet into the slot between the raft wall and the floor. This not only locks me in but allows me to lean right back as required when going down steep droppers. I paddle hard to get in the right position so I can work with the white water as it swirls around the first large rock. Timing is everything, work with the current, don't fight it. The drop off is about one meter high, maybe more. I know speed will give me the momentum to push through. I am aware of "stoppers" where a raft gets stuck in the standing wave caused by the water powering over the rocks. I lean back as much as possible while I paddle furiously, so the raft doesn't nosedive. Stoppers can be fatal.

Yes! I'm through, but straight away there are more drop-offs in front of me. No time to hesitate, procrastination is a curse. I align myself for the next one. All good again, and my confidence is rising. There is a series of smaller drop-offs then I paddle to the side to join the others. There are cheers all round as we all make it through our first real challenge. It's a great feeling.

I know there are many more challenges ahead, OMG what have I gotten myself into?! I take the time to soak in the contrasts of my wonderful surroundings which only serve to reinforce the remoteness of this place.

Chapter 5

University Life

Just as the river is evolving, so is my life. I leave school and discover life at university, in the big smoke.

Mum and Dad moved to Brisbane when I was in grade 12. Fortunately, they bought a house in St Lucia, very close to Queensland University. Great for me as it was only a push bike ride away from my lecture theatres. Even more importantly it allowed me to mingle easily with my Churchie mates who mainly ended up at Johns college at Qld Uni.

One eventful night saw five of us in a 1950's era Austin A40. We only had to drive 150 metres, from Johns college to the girls' college next door. As we drove into the girls' college, the old Austin (I can only assume the suspension was not all that good) rolled over and ended up on its roof. People, grog and various other articles went everywhere, including onto the roadway. No seatbelts of course. I was the first to get out of the car, the others were just rolling around laughing, in various positions inside the car. Girls came running down the entrance road from the college screaming and carrying on, bla, bla, bla.

After a short time, I started to smell fuel leaking, this could get serious quickly. Being the only obvious sensible person in attendance (believe that if you wish) I started yelling, 'Get out guys, get out now, I can smell fuel, she's gunna blow!'. It took a while for any reaction, and fortunately the car never blew up, and we rolled it back onto its wheels.

The old Austin was retired back to the farm out at Dalby from where my Uni mate, Ed, had borrowed it from his father. I'm not sure if we were ever forgiven, but we went out to the farm for my mates 21st and apologised to his Dad. We also conducted a memorial service in honour of the Austin, which was rusting nearby with a caved-in roof still showing the story.

Concerts were the big thing back then, with great bands lining up in one night. This particular night there was a huge lineup of artists, and we all had tickets. Men at Work, The Mentals (Mental as Anything), Bulamakanka, Red Gum to name just a few, were playing. It was a big night out. After the concert the announcer called for anyone interested to meet backstage to help the roadies pack up, $20.00 was on offer. Seeing an opportunity, I convinced some of my mates to get involved, but not in the way organisers had intended.

In front of the stage at ground level was a massive canvas mural banner displaying the names of all the bands. It was five feet high and reached right across the stage. My theory was, because they asked anyone and everyone to help, there would not be much control of who did what. Instead of going backstage for instructions, we started undoing the banner; act like you know what you're doing, right? My theory was good, and no one asked any questions. The banner may have ended up in the back of someone's car that I knew. We didn't hang around for the $20.00.

Lesson: Take your chances.

The banner mysteriously appeared at many a Saint Lucia house party that was common at the time. Certainly, a talking point, 'Where did that come from? How did it get here?' Hmmm.

Saint Lucia house parties were something else and need special mention. Queensland University is in the suburb of Saint Lucia,

Brisbane. Back in the 1980's Saint Lucia property was so much cheaper, and university students could afford to rent out a house. It was standard practice for groups to leave their college after two years and share a house in Saint Lucia together. These days Saint Lucia houses are mainly owned and occupied by rich families, so students move further afield.

Each week the usual challenge was to find out who was hosting next weekend's house party and where. Word would get around and normally well over one hundred revellers would turn up. Communication was just by word of mouth, there was no Facebook or internet. If it was you who was hosting the party, good luck. The police would invariably turn up uninvited to help out.

University days – BBQ party on rock island, 1982 (which gets submerged at high tide).

At one such party there was a huge bonfire going. Before long all the wood was burnt, and guests started attacking the wooden fence pickets for more wood. This would not end well for the tenants as the owners would eventually find out, for sure. A more creative and strategic approach was required, so I immediately stepped in to assist. 'Take every second fence pale', I insisted, 'That way the owners will never know!'.

At another party the boys started having a pissing competition. The winner was the person who could piss the furthest. So, the boys would drink excessively without relieving themselves for as long as humanly possible. Then when absolutely necessary they would take the piss, and someone would measure the reaching distance of the urine. But that's not all. For extra special effects some of the boys had earlier scoffed all the beetroot from the BBQ food so that their urine had turned a reddish colour. Only engineers could think up such technical and refined party games.

I never really took to the life of study; my mind was always wandering during lectures. Then it was a mad scramble to catch up, especially at exam times. Chemical Engineering is not an easy degree. Lectures get complex and involved, quite quickly. If you daydream in the first part of a lecture, you quickly get swamped and can't catch up by re-focussing. The lecture passes you by, and back then there was no online option. If you got lost in a subject, the textbook was the only solution. In hindsight it's a shame I didn't get more focussed during lectures. It's not all bad though, as I think you only start learning properly when you enter the workforce. University is just about teaching you how to think and learn. I was a slow learner.

Study at university was punctuated with snow skiing trips in winter and vocational work experience in industry during the summer holidays. Both great distractions. I formed great friendships during the vocational work experiences and always kept in touch for years after.

With one such group we decided to have a BBQ. The location was a bit different. We had noticed that a small rock island formed each day at low tide in the middle of the Brisbane River adjacent to Leo's college on campus. The idea was to get a dinghy, stock it up with a BBQ, firewood, food, beers, very loud music machine and go to the island at low tide. Before long we were partying, hard, the BBQ smoking away and the music, LOUD. The Leo college boys heard us and started yelling out from the riverbank. They soon returned with their golf clubs and started taking pot shots at us. A big day.

On the drive home there was not enough room in the car for everyone so I was sitting in the dinghy as it was being towed through the university streets. We went through a round-about obviously too quickly and the dinghy flew off the trailer. I went flying through the air and landed on the footpath. The comment from one of the crew in the car was, 'I turned around and saw Doug flying through the air, his sombrero still on his head!'. I must have landed gently or with a relaxed demeanor, as there were no broken bones.

Chapter 6

The Bike

There is no traffic. I am on the double lane highway travelling south into Brisbane. I open up the throttle and feel a surge of power. The noise of the wind picks up in my ears as I accelerate. 140, 160, 180 kph. I have never been this fast on the bike before, but there are no cars on the highway, and I feel safe. Up ahead in the distance I see a car I am closing in on, so I slow down to 110 kph. As I pass, I take particular notice of the occupants, as I don't want a speeding fine. The driver wears a floral Hawaiian shirt, and the passenger has the seat completely reclined and has a newspaper over his head. I put my university education to work and do a quick risk assessment. I determine they are 'friendlies'. The possibility of having an accident does not feature in my risk assessment. I draw away and when I'm well clear, crank the bike again.

I start to enter heavy traffic and slow right down. I hear the siren and look to my right. The passenger's seat is no longer reclined, and they are waving me over. They are flashing a police sign at me. Shit.

"We had you clocked at 140 kph. Any faster and we could impound your bike." Hawaiian shirt man is not happy. What can I say, I am actually feeling lucky they don't know the full extent of it. Next time I must refine my method of risk assessment.

I always enjoyed motorbike riding. I started with a 125 cc trail bike which my Mum tolerated. When I turned up at home with a 750cc bike, my Mum was in a state of shock. She insisted I do two things.

1. I enrolled in a defensive riding course. I did this and it was a great move. I strongly recommend this for any motor bike rider. It probably saved me from at least one serious accident. Also, during the day you get to do fast laps at Lakeside speedway.

2. That I accompany her brother to the orthopaedic ward at the Princess Alexandra hospital. Mum's brother was an orthopaedic surgeon and told Mum his ward was full of injured and crippled motorbike riders. Mum thought it would be a good idea if I accompanied Uncle Bill on his ward rounds and talk to all the injured patients. I refused.

Two of my bikie mates talked me into a quick trip from Brisbane to the Atherton tablelands, 1700 km away. It was a 5-day getaway to blow out the cobwebs. Two days up, a day in Atherton which was hometown for one of them, then 2 days back. We were riding just north of Innisfail at night in the rain, on a windy road at the end of a long day. The car in front of me was towing a trailer. I didn't realise the brake lights on the trailer didn't work. As the car braked the gap closed quickly. By the time I realised it was so close it was too late. I couldn't brake hard because of the wet road. My top-quality soft compound Pirelli tyres saved me as I just pulled up in time without skidding out of control. The learnings from the defensive riding course came through. It was this course that taught me how to brake hard and to ensure I carried the best tyres available. Thanks Mum!

I have since enrolled all my family in a defensive driving course, also highly recommended.

When I finally finished my degree in June 1982, professional work opportunities were extremely limited, and my university results were not spectacular. So, I went travelling for several months to southern Australia on my Honda 750 K6 motor bike. I had all my possessions on a rack on the back and stayed in youth hostels (YHA).

All went well until I remembered regaining consciousness on the side of the road. There was a semi-trailer parked nearby, and a truckie looking guy was standing over me asking if I was ok. Apparently, he came around the corner and saw me sliding down the road. I don't remember what happened, I must have been concussed. The side of my helmet was all grazed and I had skin off both knees. Anyway, he called for assistance on his truck's VHF (very high frequency) radio and the ambulance took me to hospital. I checked out as ok. Because of the cold I was very heavily rugged up and I think this may have saved some serious loss of skin. Fortunately the bike wasn't badly damaged.

I was soon on my way again and worked my way back home via the Snowy Mountains. Despite being a bit cold sometimes (riding over the mountains as the snow was melting in August) it was a fantastic trip, lots of great roads going wherever they took me. True freedom.

Biker holidays – Honda 750K6 circa 1982

I was still, however, an expert at being a nuisance. A group of us regularly ventured over the NSW border to Hastings Point and Pottsville. On one trip we were partying at my friends' parents beach house right on the beach at Pottsville, a truly great location. About 2.00 am the party was waning as people were starting to get some sleep, or so they thought. Too early by my reckoning. I managed to get the bike up several steps and into the lounge room and fired it up, revving it hard in neutral. Noisy to say the least, but it restarted proceedings!

I had several great trips on the bike and managed to survive intact.

PART TWO

The Turbulent Years
Crazy Days

Spectacular side streams and waterfalls continue to provide energy to the river. They transform it from a river with youthful enthusiasm into a strong formidable force to be respected by all who venture within.

My somewhat adventurous pursuits seem to be reinforcing a risk-taker attitude. Success grows one's self-confidence. I take larger risks, I get closer to the edge, the cliffs get higher……

Stuffed – Big day of portaging around rapids

Chapter 7

Fun times in the Burdekin...the rapids are escalating

Driving into the Burdekin (population of the main town of Ayr about 7,000) on 3rd February 1984 was a pivotal point of time in my life. I remember how small and lifeless it looked that Sunday afternoon as I drove down the main street. The place looked deserted. Nothing was happening. I drove around for a while, checking out places like the golf club and the pubs, trying to get some inspiration that everything was going to work out. I failed. The experience was daunting, especially as I did not know anyone within 300 km of this place. I ignored my feelings and got to organising somewhere to live.

This was it as there were no other job offers available for me at the time, The engineering industry was at a low ebb. Would I survive this little, quiet town? Maybe I could liven things up!!!

On the drive to Ayr, I stayed with friends in Gladstone, and they introduced me to Hash House Harriers. These are drinkers with a running problem, who are part of a great world-wide social networking organisation. People from all walks of life party together with loose rules on what you can't do, that are aimed at making you drink more. Everyone in Hash, no matter your job or profession, party on the same page. Everyone is equal. Everyone gets on with each other, this is not optional.

I soon found out there was a newly formed Hash group in Ayr, and I had an instant friend circle. Off to a great start. Hash was/is on every Monday, irrespective of where you are. A special feature of the Burdekin Hash was the can night. This occurred regularly. Everyone would bring a can of food, no dog food allowed. Every can was emptied into a big vat and cooked up with mince. It was surprising how nice it tasted, especially after a few "down downs"!

Each week an article would appear in the local paper, the Ayr Advocate, describing the run and after party in detail. The article was normally fairly loose with the truth and often diverged into international politics, or something else even more vaguely related to the event. I often had the locals (who were not even in Hash) tell me the only reason they bought the local paper was to read the Hash notes because they were so funny and/or thought provoking. I have included some of the articles written by Hash Scribe (yours truly), at the end of this memoir for context. Enjoy. This may have been the start of my writing career!

Every year we would all go to an island resort in the Whitsundays for a weekend away. This became a very much anticipated event on the Hash calendar.

Over the years, quite a few romances started from Hash, and at least 9 marriages resulted as well; mine included. Incredible statistics considering that over the years, maybe a total of 80 people were part of Burdekin Hash! My wife and I still have several close friends from the Hash days, 40 years prior.

One of the Hash guys, Rotary (that was his Hash nickname), was a crop-dusting pilot who had access to a Cessna. He took us in his plane to weekend Hash activities in other towns. Always a great weekend away where the host town celebrates milestones like their 21st run or 100th run etc. These events made going to work on Monday difficult.

One time a friend of Rotary's (also a crop duster pilot) took me up in his crop duster and we did a few circuits. Simply amazing. Under power lines and skimming across the lagoons with the wheels touching the water.

Another time I was sitting at home one Sunday morning and the phone rang, 'Hey Sox, what are you doing for lunch?'. 'Not much Rotary, what's on?'

'We're going to Brampton Island for lunch, are you interested?' Well, no need to ask twice. Brampton was still an operating resort off Mackay at the time, about 1.5 hours in the Cessna. How good was it to fly over the Whitsunday islands with the sun dazzling off the sparkling blue waters. I could clearly see the islands where I had explored in the charter yachts. Returning home we went low over the water, and I turned around to see the ripples created by the wheels touching the water, again. Bloody crop duster pilots! But it was exhilarating!

I learnt to scuba dive whilst in Ayr. The waters off Ayr are a diving mecca.

We are anchored off Ayr above the wreck of the Yongala ship. This is a world-renowned dive site, one of the best. The Yongala rests in about 25 meters of water and is a protected marine area, no fishing allowed.

I slowly descend and immediately the fish life is just incredible. I have dived in several locations along the great barrier reef, and this is extreme, next level. All around me there are what I describe as walls of fish, that is, so many fish that they form a large wall in front of you, blocking further visibility through them. I lay on my back, relax and look up through the crystal-clear water, soaking up the wonderland before my eyes. The brilliant bright colours of purple, yellow and all the other colours of the rainbow. Fish of all sizes from tiny specs to large gropers. They are just drifting around right in front of me, they have no fear.

Continuing down, the wreck is clearly visible, lying on its side. I can make out the complete structure. It is still intact despite having sunk in 1911. Coral is everywhere, and seaweed growth is waving in the ocean current like giant tentacles.

Just as I am settling into the rhythm of swimming amongst this amazing fish life, my buddy (people always dive in pairs as a safety measure) grabs my flipper from behind to get my attention. I turn around to see her signalling that she has run out of air, way too soon. We have been trained to consciously relax and breathe slowly to conserve the precious air, but clearly my buddy has been taken away with the moment. We are now 25 metres below surface level, which is deep enough to take things seriously when something goes wrong. We have a second mouthpiece attached to our air tanks to handle this exact issue. I quickly get it to her, so she can breathe and settle down before we must surface together, very slowly, so as not to get the bends. (Getting the bends can be deadly, and we are a long way from nowhere.) This involves slowly letting air into my buoyancy control vest, then releasing the air back out as we rise. (The vest expands as you rise because the water pressure reduces. The vest is used to control your speed of ascent.) I have never been in this situation before, and I don't have time to procrastinate. It is a tricky procedure that requires intricate timing using two control valves. I get it wrong. Before I know what is happening, we torpedo out of the water together at breakneck speed. I surface to about waist level with the momentum of the vertical speed. Now I am petrified that we will get the bends. All our training had been about, 'Rise slowly from deep water, VERY slowly!'. We must have been too shallow for the bends to be an issue, and we survive the ordeal. Relief sweeps through me.

Another time I was diving out on the reef. It is normal for a few sharks to be around. They don't normally bother a scuba diver because you are floating around calmly and not giving off distress signals. However this time, more and more sharks were accumulating and swimming around faster like something was happening. I was reaching my risk tolerance level and went back to the boat, slithering in as quickly as I could whilst giving off minimum distress-like signals. I couldn't believe my eyes; here in the charter boat was a guy who had decided to start fishing while we were down diving! No wonder the sharks were gathering around. Idiot!

The Burdekin turned out to offer so much. Every night there was a social or a serious sport that one could get involved in. Our group joined night soccer, indoor cricket, squash and volleyball. Day time pursuits were sailing, water skiing, yachting, fishing and golf.

The water ski club in Ayr was fantastic. It is set in a beautiful location on a lagoon with giant rain trees along the foreshore. The club was very well organised which resulted in cheap skiing behind the club boat. We skied on wooden planks which are just that, bare bits of wood with no bindings and no fins. Quite tricky. Then we would step off these and barefoot ski. Barefoot skiing is difficult to learn because you can't start off slow, or you sink. So, it is all or nothing, learning at 4o kph. Mostly a bruising experience whilst learning. We enjoyed a great social atmosphere which was also well organised.

Golfing in Ayr requires a special mention. Every month a hash sub-group participated in a very social team-golf competition. The ambrose golf format allows for four people to play together, each time hitting from where the team's best shot landed. Ayr golf club ran an ambrose competition for many years. It was extremely popular with about 120 people hitting off each month. Beer tents were spread throughout the course to ensure no one was ever thirsty. This plan worked well. This competition was far more popular than the serious members' golfing competitions.

Each team had to have a team name. Our team was called OPC, short for 'optimum piss content'. Our theory was that golf is very much a mind game. That is, the mind interferes with performance, because people overthink the sport. We believed that if you could dull the brain so it influenced your game less, you could play better. A certain level of relaxation was required. To continue the logic, if you drank alcohol whilst playing, your game improved. This is only to a point, though, because eventually you fall over and cannot play at all. (Measured experience) To continue the logic further, there must be an optimum blood alcohol level for peak golfing performance. We did think about mathematically spreadsheeting this in a systematic factorial scientific experiment but were never sober enough to carry it out. Our team motto was what I was most proud of; 'You don't know you're there until you've gone too far!'. Love it. To continue further on the beer theme, our shirt colour scheme represented a pot of beer, amber colour on the lower 90% and white on the top. A refined touch that I doubt many people understood.

Overall, there was never a dull moment and I thoroughly enjoyed my time up north. Who would have thought? Little did I realise how fantastic my time in Ayr would become, and how much of a life-changing experience this would prove to be.

Lesson: When in doubt, take the chance.

Chapter 8

The Thunder Rush portage

We knew about this portage; our guidebook mentioned it. Attempting to raft through Thunder Rush rapids would be fatal, no doubt about it.

We can hear the noise long before we get to it. That's a good thing, as we don't want to accidently raft this rapid. We pull to the side and tie our rafts up firmly. We don't want them going down the rapids accidently, with or without a passenger. We scamper up the rocks to see the lay of the land, and the river. We are amazed by the grandness of the rocks, the canyon, the ferocity of the waterfalls and the foam and mist rising from the noise. Everywhere is wet from the constant mist.

We look around for the portage trail. That can't be right, it looks so steep, muddy and slippery. It tracks up beside the cliff wall at an alarming angle. We return to the rafts and start the long process of undoing everything. Barrels, tents, backpacks, cooking gear, etc. etc. Then we deflate the rafts and tie them up in a manageable way, so we can strap them on our backs. We all select a lighter load for the first trip, so we can get used to the trek and what it means.

Off we set. The track is immediately steep, and so slippery. Fortunately, trees hang off the cliff wall. We use these to literally pull ourselves up from one ledge to the next. We have been told that people have fallen to their death on these trails. We consciously move slowly and carefully.

We eventually get to the top and jettison our packs. They now seem so heavy. Again we scout around for the best path forward, and find the trail that will take us back down to the river, downstream of the noise. Going down proves worse as it is not as easy to use the trees for stability. Finally, we get back to the river. Only three more trips to go to get the rest of our equipment!

There are many rapids that require portaging along the Franklin. Thunder Rush takes about six hours and is one of the more demanding. Some portages are low level, and some can be accomplished by "roping" the rafts along the edges of the river, but this can be more risky. Roping is where you tie long ropes to the front and the back of the raft and two people do their best to 'guide' the raft through the rocks along the edge of the river. Even a roped raft can get stuck or lodged in a submerged log, or stopper. It can then be a big problem to rescue the raft with all the precious equipment in it, before it gets lost in the foam.

Chapter 9

The Great Ravine

We were in the Great Ravine, a series of death-defying rapids with names like 'the Churn', 'Thunder Rush', 'The Cauldron' and 'Corkscrew'. The Dean and Hawkins party, who in 1959, after several attempts were the first to successfully descend the Franklin, took six days to complete this stretch of river. They called it 'Deception Gorge' and they were not at all pleased with the effort it required. Johnson Dean recounts in his book 'Shooting the Franklin' as they were destined for another miserable night in a rough campsite, 'I wished I had never encountered this hideous defile.' He goes on to describe how Hawkins nearly drowned in this section of the river in one of their earlier failed attempts.

We had just spent the whole morning portaging around Thunder Rush and had stopped for a rest on the edge of the river just below the worst of the rapids.

The roar is deafening, it fills my ears. I have to yell to be heard. I can feel the moisture as it clings to my skin. We turn around to survey the rapids upstream. Unbelievably we see two guys crawling over the rocks at the end of the rapids. They are each carrying a kayak. They must have worked their way through and over the upstream rocks instead of portaging. That could not have been easy or safe! This was the first we had seen of them.

Roping around rapids, easier than portaging as rafts don't need to be unpacked.

The guys are now poised on the giant rock formations upstream from where we stand. They still have one set of rapids to negotiate. They are gesturing frantically to each other. Their fate is cast, there is no way back upstream against the flow. They are hopelessly trapped. Why didn't they walk around the cliff trail like we had? Between them and relative safety stood two giant rocks. Huge quantities of water rushed between the two rocks, each rock the size of a small bus. To jump into the turmoil below would surely be fatal. Unbelievably they start to manoeuvre the first of their two kayaks to bridge the 2-meter gap between the rocks. With all their combined strength they manage the feat. Slowly and determinedly, the taller guy eases himself onto the teetering kayak. It is wobbling as he inches forward in this incredible attempt to get to the downstream rock. His long scraggly wet hair is blowing in the wind formed by the churning water, creating a spray and mist that rises up past the mountainous surroundings. If he can get to the next rock, downstream, he stands half a chance of surviving. A torrent of water is tearing just inches below him as it erupts between the rocks.

After what seemed like an eternity, he scrambles onto the second rock. Long hair man retrieves his kayak by pulling it onto the downstream rock where he crouches. He then looks back at his friend. Now what? It took their combined strength to position the first kayak; there is no way one person could achieve the same feat. Unperturbed, the second guy starts to position the next kayak as the bridge so he can follow in the same way. He is shorter but stockier and I can see his muscles bulging with the effort. His red hair is just protruding from the safety stack hat he is wearing. He looks extremely fit. Despite a totally desperate effort, he is not able to achieve this plan on his own. His mate looks on helplessly from the downstream rock, pointing and gesturing to no avail. His long mane is blowing across his face as he gestures. Then it happens, the inevitable. The second kayak slips from the grasp of red hair man, and it slides into the churning water which is erupting between the two huge rocks. We watch; spellbound, in horror. Time is critical as the kayak is now getting washed downstream in the wild unforgiving rapids. Red hair man crouches onto his knees, his arms cradling his head in despair. I am sharing his fear, there is no safe option here. His kayak is gone, it's just him and the elements. Slowly he starts to compose himself and looks around. His only option is to try to jump to the next rock, over two metres away. This is not a good option, but he has no other. The rocks look slippery. The saying, 'between a rock and a hard place', comes to mind. He is now walking back to get a good run up, but there is very little room. No way. His short stature will not help. Then it happens. Getting as much speed up as he can, he takes the ultimate leap of faith. His foot just lands at the near edge of the downstream rock and slips. He ricochets off into the water. He is washed around the rock and disappears in the froth. Without hesitation the long hair man jumps into the water with his kayak, using it as a float. Where is red hair man? His mate is looking around frantically. Finally, after what seems like minutes, he appears from the turmoil and starts coughing furiously. Long hair man works his way over and helps his mate onto his own kayak. They manage to make it to the side of the river. There is hope after all.

'Why didn't you portage around the rapids?', I ask red hair man when our paths cross soon after on the next portaging track. The question is as obvious as it is intriguing. I am thinking they had made a dangerous mistake in not reading their guidebook properly, hence becoming unintentionally trapped. Note: There was no luxury of satellite navigation in 1984. *'We're going for the record', long hair man replies (red hair man is still sputtering).*

Well, that's a stupid way to die, I think, but I hold my tongue. 'No one has ever rafted the Franklin in 24 hours', he continues, 'and we're going for the record. We started before first light today and we can save so much time by not portaging.'

Right really, I ponder. It had taken us 4 days to do what they had accomplished in half a day, but their approach was very risky. By only taking one day they can avoid taking most of the supplies and equipment a normal expedition requires. Everything they needed was tucked away inside their kayaks. 'Good luck!' I remark. In no time at all they are on their way again. I never found out if they succeeded. I didn't hear of any deaths on our return to civilization, so I assume they survived.

At night, as we cook up our meal on the burner (there was no dry wood for a campfire), we reflect on the day's events. Today we saw the river at its craziest; packed full of youthful energy and exuberance. Today we saw risk taking on the edge.

Some of my friends say I am a risk taker. I'm not so sure. Everything is relative. I see the two crazy guys in the kayaks and my crazy scale gets re-adjusted. What drives people to take risks? What stops people from taking risks? Why do some people have more gumption than others, and set different limits? Why do some people just coast along in life whilst others seek every experience imaginable? Why do some people need to have an unplanned near-death experience to start really living, whilst others create their own near-death experiences?

I am developing the premise that more risk equals more fun. I reflect on some of the crazier things I have done in my life and why I have taken risks.

Beautiful side streams add to the river's strength and character.

Chapter 10

Jail Time

The Ayr town clock is the landmark in town. It is about 8 metres high and is in the middle of the main intersection. It's about 1.00 am. Blood alcohol level unknown. I am about one third of the way up when I look down and go pale. It is not the height taking my breath away. It is the police officer looking up at me. I know him and he doesn't like me, not at all. Constable Parland is the same cop who tried to nab me for driving under the influence a few weeks previously and failed (more on this shortly).

Not good. I jump down, spotting the taxi rank nearby. I walk briskly past Constable Parland and jump in the nearest taxi. The driver has a huge ear to ear smile on his dial. Funny for some, I think. 'Quickly', I say to him, 'Can't you see I'm in deep shit, get me the fuck outta here. Now!'. Definitely a Thunder Rush moment in time!

Up for the challenge he speeds off leaving old mate wondering if he should take a chance on arresting me again. Too slow. The taxi driver's smile gets even bigger!

I often get asked, 'Hey Sox, there's a rumour going around that you climbed the clock. Is it true? Why did you do it?'.

Simple answer, 'Because it's there, and because no one else has'.

A few weeks prior to "the incident at the town clock in the nighttime", I was returning to get my towel that I had left at a "beach party" where I had just spent several hours. The cops pulled me over, saying I was meandering, not driving in a straight line. In those days they needed a reason to pull you over, there was no random breath testing. You could also refuse to do the breath test; however, this was a risky strategy. You could end up getting the highest-level blood alcohol content (BAC) charge if you refused a breath test and were subsequently found guilty in court because there was a valid reason for the cops to pull you over. It is a risk versus reward conundrum.

The infamous Ayr town clock

After being arrested, I had caused a ruckus in the Ayr jailhouse because I refused to sign their bullshit paperwork and refused a breath test as well. Actually, I did sign it, with an X. Apparently not allowable according to Constable Parland. No sense of humour! So, I spent a night in the big house for my sins. Complimentary breakfast refused. Lift home also refused.

Late that night my partner in alleged crime, Ross, arrived in my faithful HQ Holden (more on my HQ later). I could just see him over the top of the jail cell windowsill when I looked through the reinforced bars. I remembered a western from when I was a kid and recalled the line where they used a horse to tear out the bars and run to freedom. So, continuing on that theme I yelled out, 'Hey Rosco, back the HQ up and throw me a rope, we'll pull the bars out and be off'! The copper standing near Ross on the footpath, Constable Parland (who else?), thought I was serious – no sense of humour. Ross got told, 'Go any closer and you'll be joining him for the night.'

It took me two days in court to demonstrate my innocence. I got off on a technicality. We (my solicitor and I) were able to show the magistrate that I was not actually weaving, I was following the bitumen road, driving like a sober person. The edges were not straight or aligned with the footpath. We even took the magistrate out to the roads in question and showed him what we meant! He understood. This meant the police had no legitimate reason to arrest me.

The look on constable Parland's face, when the verdict was read out, was gold. So that's why I was concerned when I looked down from the clock tower and saw him again. I could see revenge written all over his face.

As I said it took two days to prove my innocence. After day one, the hearing had to be adjourned until there was a spare day in the Ayr courts. The magistrate set the date and read it out. There was something about the date that got me thinking, it rang a faint bell in the back of my brain. Then I remembered. I leaned over to my solicitor and whispered, 'I can't do that day, I have an appointment in the Cairns courthouse that I can't change!'. I must give my solicitor 10/10 for composure. Calm as you like he just stood up and said, 'Excuse me your Honor, my client has to appear in Cairns court on that date, could we please explore other options?' A wry smirk appeared on the magistrate's face, and we sorted out a new date. My lawyer soon gave up law to become a long serving federal Senator.

So, the Cairns courthouse proceedings.

Now, that one was much more serious – three years in the big house were on offer. An extra year because the alleged offence 'occurred in the nighttime'. Serious rapids. I was nervous. At least they'd feed me this time.

Ross (my partner in alleged crime from the Ayr drink driving incident) and I had been over to Fitzroy Island off Cairns for a cabaret. It was a big night, and I must confess we drew a bit of attention. Anyway, we didn't think much of it at the time, but as we got off the ferry back in Cairns and got into our car, we noticed the island staff nearby. As it turns out they were observing us closely and must have written down the rego of our car as we got in.

The next day we were about 30 minutes south of Cairns driving back to the Burdekin, and the cops pulled us over. Ross says, 'What's going on here, I wasn't speeding?'

So, the cops get us out of the car, start yelling, 'Take your sunglasses off, hands on the bonnet, what's your name?' and bla bla bla for a while. Then they take us in separate cars back to the Cairns police station. They continued to keep us apart. We eventually found out we were up on a charge of 'killing and maiming clams in the nighttime', and had been placed on a state-wide police alert.

It's a long story, but essentially, they said we were dropping pebbles into giant clams in a display tank on Fitzroy Island, and the clams were dead or dying. Apparently, clams have very small digestive systems, and don't like pebbles!

This is where it gets tricky. The cops say our best way forward is simply to plead guilty. If we do this there are two advantages.

1. Proceedings can be finalised simply and easily in the Ayr courthouse when we get home.

2. And secondly, we'll only be charged as per the price of clam meat where it is commonly sold, in Thailand, for $5.00 per kg.

If we plead not guilty, we must return to Cairns, face lengthy court proceedings, and take our chances on the verdict. Pleading guilty seemed so straight forward. It was economically and pragmatically the best option so we took it and left town. The case was to be referred to the Ayr courthouse at a later date. What could possibly go wrong!?

Upon returning to Ayr, we organised a solicitor to hear our 'straightforward' case. Now significantly, just prior to this, there were people in Adelaide who had been stabbing kangaroos in the Adelaide Zoo. It made headlines nationwide at the time and there was bad public sentiment about the event. Our Ayr solicitor took one look at our charge, and said, 'Do you realise you are effectively on the same charge as the people in Adelaide? You could go to jail for 3 years if you're proven guilty. You need to plead not guilty!'. There was no mention of this in Cairns from the detectives questioning us! We had been verballed! (Coaxed into pleading guilty with misleading statements when we weren't guilty.) These rapids were becoming very turbulent, we needed to portage! To say I was worried was an understatement!

So, we changed our plea to not guilty and organised a barrister in Cairns. There was not much need for discussion. It was obvious what we needed to do. This was probably one of the most important decisions I have ever made. A right call. Minimise the risk!

We then had to travel back to Cairns to set a date for our committal hearing. As Christmas was approaching, a date was set for the following year in the Cairns courts. This was the date that clashed with my second day in the Ayr courthouse.

The next day I was driving down to Brisbane on annual leave, and I was listening to the ABC national news at 6am. Low and behold I hear my name being mentioned and I'm all over the news. I was never sure if my parents heard the news, but they never questioned me about it.

The day of reckoning finally arrived and we're sitting in the Cairns courthouse. The atmosphere was palpable. Jail scared me, a lot.

My partner in the alleged crime, Ross (who else?), seemed to be on top of it and tried to lighten the mood. He was lead singer in a rock band. When the judge walked in, the big reel to reel tape recorder in front of us started spinning via remote control. Ross's quick-witted comment flawed me, 'Hey Sox, what's it like to be cutting your first album?'. 'Shut up you idiot', I thought. Too much, too loud. The judge was sitting only five metres away. Luckily, I don't think he heard the remark. It was important that we appeared as credible characters.

We were up on a charge of, 'Killing and maiming clams in the nighttime.', which means we had intentionally tried to kill the clams. This was far from the truth. The judge soon worked this out and dismissed the charge, thank goodness. A close call! How different my life would have been if not for the advice from our Ayr solicitor. A huge dam in the river of my life was narrowly avoided. We were not at all impressed with the deceitful way the Cairns detectives had verballed us initially.

When I got back to work, my mill Manager was interested in how I went. 'No worries, Dave, I got off, all good!' I replied.

'Ah well, I guess that makes it two out of two Sox!', came the reply. It was good to have a boss with a sense of humour.

Thinking back, I now realise this time was peak rapids in my life. Too close to the edge! Let's call this one a precipice. These experiences were slowly teaching me that there are limits to what society deems acceptable and I started to settle down a bit, but not totally.

Chapter 11

Disaster! Bubble bubble toil and trouble

We can just see the lead rafters in the distance through the rising mist, making it successfully through the white water and pulling off to the side. They give us the thumbs up, but it doesn't look convincing.

Immediately prior to inevitable disaster

I am going through the training instructions in my mind. Use the current, don't fight it. Lean back. Feet first downstream if you fall in. Watch out for submerged trees if you fall in. Avoid large stoppers. Look for the grab rope if you fall in. Too much information, and I know there will be no time to think if I capsize. I don't have time to take in the incredible scenery all around us. 'What can possibly go wrong?'. Yeah right!

That's it, I'm all in!

Here I go, it's my turn, and I'm petrified. I pull the straps tight on my life jacket and helmet. I wedge my feet into the side walls hard so I can lean right back and get purchase with the paddles in the water. We are in one person rafts. I can't rely on anyone else. It's me only. I start paddling, hard. The stopper is right in front of me. It is much larger close up compared to what I saw from the bank. I have been told stoppers can be fatal. They can be formed by submerged logs or rocks that create an undercurrent of water with a strong downflow. This is what keeps you submerged. The only chance of getting out is to try to kick yourself off the rock bottom, if it's not too deep. Down I go, into the stopper. It is scary and exhilarating at the same time. The raft starts to flip. I lean back even more to try and counter the forces. I fail. Water erupts in my face.

Water and bubbles are all around me, the shock of the cold taking my breath away. Did I have time to take a breath before I fell in, I can't remember? Do I have time to be nervous or scared; no. I reach up and feel the raft above me, but I am still under water struggling for lack of breath. I feel trapped beneath the raft. Try to remain calm. Conserve energy. I eventually find the side rope that is attached all the way around the raft. Using it to pull me up, I can finally take a breath and suck in some glorious air, all the time trying to keep my head above the churning water. I stick with the raft, moving rapidly downstream while getting bounced around violently. I start to focus on what I must do. The current is spinning me around. Training kicks in and I swing my feet downstream. This way if there are any shallow rocks I can deflect my body with my feet and not my head. I am bouncing around, furiously, hardly in any form of control. I push off a large rock, trying frantically not to get sucked into another stopper. I can see the lead rafters just downstream on the side of the river. I do not know what rapids are further downstream, and don't want to find out the hard way. The lead rafters are yelling out to me, trying to get my attention. I can see the throw rope in his hand, poised ready. As I get closer, the rope uncoils above me; a great throw, thank God. I manage to catch the throw rope with one hand, not letting go of the raft with the other hand, and they pull me safely to the side.

Now I know what it's like to fall in. Adrenalin is still pumping through my body. I am too revved up to feel the cold. What on earth have I signed up for here? What lays ahead for me in this chaos? I know there is no way back. 'Is everybody having fun?!'

The rapids end suddenly, for the time being. A temporary reprieve.

The river now flows deep and still. Towering canyon rock walls reach skyward abruptly from the river. Cliffs reflect in the clear calm waters. The river is relentless, calving its way through the terrain. What a contrast to the rapids! Surreal does not fully describe this setting. The thick moss covers the rocks. Trees spring out precariously from the cliff tops. A light mist filters through the trees. The noise from the rapids slowly recedes into the distance as we drift downstream into the emerging silence.

Chapter 12

Travel

Just as the Franklin meanders through the mountains and valleys, I find myself exploring the world, investigating each nook and cranny; taking the risks where and when my curiosity demands. What is around the corner? Are there rapids? Is there danger? Will I be pleasantly surprised?

It was what the Yanks call a blue bird day. It means a perfect day for skiing, fresh powder snow on the slopes, no wind and no clouds. Too good a day to report for work at the casino. We are skiing in Squaw Valley, Lake Tahoe, California, the venue of the 1960 Winter Olympics. I had caught a series of gondolas and chair lifts up the slopes, and I am now close to the top. In the distance I can see the magic blue lake waters sparkling in the sun. Further over is the string of ski resorts on the other side of the lake where the pale white snow-capped mountains merge into the horizon.

I am approaching the legendary double black diamond run called KT22. That's code for the only way down is total commitment doing 22 kick turns to reach the bottom. A kick turn is where you flick from side to side in an attempt to slow your speed down the mountain. It is too steep to ski gently. Ski runs use a colour code to inform skiers of the level of difficulty. Starting from easy (green circle) to blue square (intermediate) to black diamond (expert, difficult) to double black diamond (expert level, extremely difficult, slope > 45 degrees, very narrow path). KT22 was part of the ski runs that were used in the Olympics. It's a head rush to experience this sort of skiing. I approach the edge at the top and have an oh-shit moment. It's so steep I can't see over the edge except for the odd rock sticking out of the slope. I am hesitating, thinking I should try to bail out i.e. backtrack and take a gentler ski run, i.e. be sensible. The terrain makes it quite difficult to back track, and skiers are cueing up behind me waiting to take off. I can feel their urgency. Trepidation eclipses excitement. The guy behind me yells out, 'Are you going or not?'

View of Lake Tahoe from ski slopes.

Nothing ventured, nothing gained, and with a deep breath and a push on the stocks I am off! A great start to another day in the USA! God bless America!

Lesson: When in doubt, take the plunge!

(In March 1982, one month after I left Tahoe, seven people died in an avalanche at Alpine Meadows resort, one of the other places we frequented at the time. This followed 100 inches of snow in a short period of time. This year, 2024, I saw reports that Squaw Valley's KT22 was hit by another avalanche).

I took an extra six months to finish my chemical engineering degree because I under-estimated the workload required to pass. (I tell people I was enjoying it too much to finish it in the regulation four years.) After the first year of just passing each subject, I thought I had it neatly worked out in regards to how to minimise the study required to pass, and hence maximise the partying. The problem was I didn't realise they stepped up the study load in second year; I had missed the email! So, I failed too many subjects which pushed out my studies by another semester. I hear you saying, 'But emails were not invented in 1979'. My point exactly!

This ended up being a blessing in disguise, as it enabled me to go on a "Kultural" exchange working tour of the United States for 3 months at the end of my fourth year, as I was still classified as a student. The work was organised through the university and provided an opportunity for students to experience another country, and for that country to learn a little bit about Australia. It worked well, with the work experience organised in advance of the trip. There was much opportunity for the student to get immersed in another culture. There were over 20 students participating in the year I went, and we were assigned to various locations throughout the USA. I was lucky and went to Cal Neva casino at Lake Tahoe with six other students. It is on the border of California and Nevada, with the border literally cutting through the swimming pool and the lounge/gambling room. Gambling is legal in Nevada, but not in California. This working holiday proved to be one of the best adventures I've had.

When I was at Cal Neva it was owned by a 90-year-old man, and it was strongly rumoured he was dating one of the cocktail waitresses. I don't recall if he was married. Soon after I left, the local papers reported that he was convicted of tampering with the poker machine odds. He was a risk taker.

It was strongly rumoured that Cal Neva was mafia central when Frank Sinatra was at his prime and performed in the showroom. Frank was a major owner in Cal Neva casino at the time. It was his favourite haunt. There are many fascinating stories detailing what went down at Cal Neva. Most famous is the legend about President Kennedy and Marilyn Monroe.

Marylin Monroe's favoured cottage at Cal Neva. A convenient tunnel system connected it to other cottages.

Besides the high-rise accommodation looking out over the lake, there are numerous cottages. They are connected via tunnels, in fact there are tunnels everywhere. You could still walk through them as part of the tunnel tour when I took my family there for a holiday in 2008. So, as the rumour goes, Marilyn would be in one cottage, and the Pres in another. Part way through the night the Pres would go for a tunnel walk and end up at Marilyn's cottage. This is the legend, anyway, as told in the tunnel tour at Cal Neva.

So, history alleges (through documentaries) that there was a link between the mafia, the Kennedys and Frank Sinatra. (One of JFK's sisters was married to one of Frank Sinatra's Rat Pack.) Prior to JFK's election, JFK allegedly rang Sinatra and asked that he get the mafia to ring their union associates and get their members to vote for JFK (it would not have been a smart move for JFK to ring the mafia directly). The union membership consisted of a significant proportion of the voting people at the time. The rest is history.

The other legend is that the gambling tables at Cal Neva would sometimes spread over to the Californian side of the casino (allegedly). When the FBI stormed the casino, the bad guys would scamper into the tunnels to escape. A quick internet search gives you the details.

Frank sold his share in the casino when its reputation developed to such an extent that it was fouling his image.

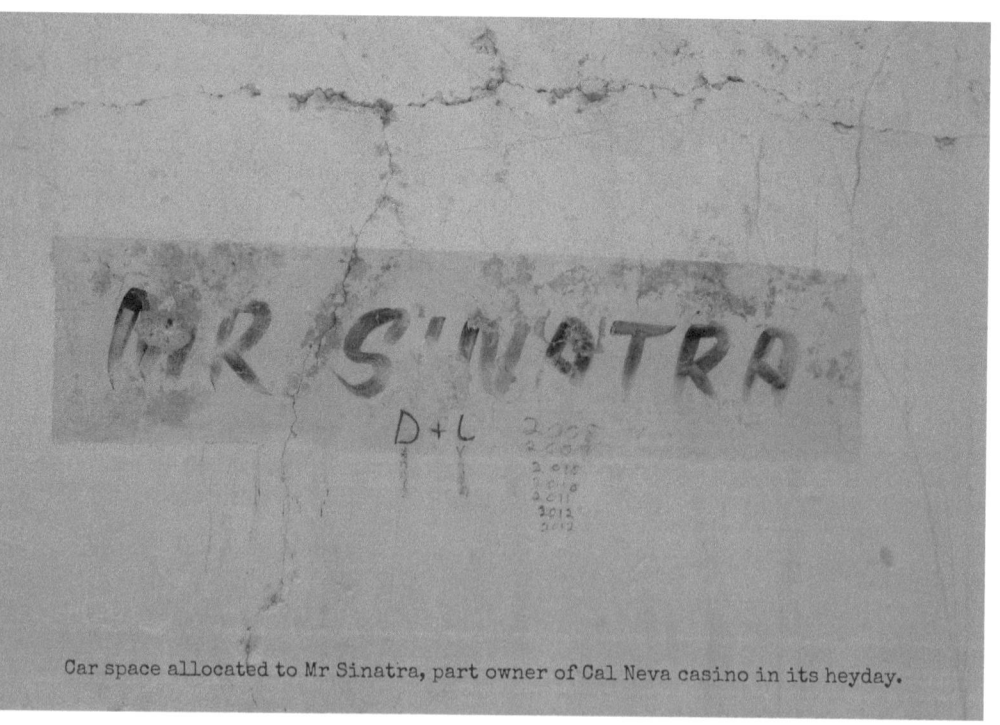

Car space allocated to Mr Sinatra, part owner of Cal Neva casino in its heyday.

We spent three months at Cal Neva. The four Australian girls in our group were allotted jobs as cocktail waitresses on the afternoon shift and we three guys did odd jobs during the day. The routine for the boys was work during the day, then sit around the gaming tables on afternoon shift. The girls would keep bringing us cocktails, which were free if you gambled, or pretended to gamble. When the girls finished their afternoon shift, we'd all go out. There were fantastic shows and cabarets each night at all the casinos around Lake Tahoe. We'd normally get back home close to sunrise.

View of Lake Tahoe from restaurant where I worked at Cal Neva casino.

The casinos never stopped and offered a cheap breakfast. If the weather was good, we'd go snow skiing for the day, if not, we'd report to work. Our jobs weren't that important, so we had flexibility about when we showed up for work. We also had a great relationship with the personnel manager who was very understanding. The plan was great; however it left me little time for sleep.

The Go-Go's are playing loud, very loud. The girls are dancing on the bed, jumping up and down like it's a trampoline, yelling out, "We got the beat", in tune with the music. Earlier they were using the mattress to toboggan down the snow embankments just outside the door. We are in our chalet which is on site at Cal Neva. The odd empty champagne bottle is getting thrown out the window and landing on the chalet next door. Oops. Suddenly there is a loud knock on the door. I open it expecting some more Yankie friends, but I instead see a well-dressed and fit looking guy who I don't know. He gets straight to the point, 'I am a bodyguard looking after my client in the chalet next door, and he can't sleep. You need to wrap this up, now'. As he is speaking his hand casually pushes his coat to the side revealing a six-shooter hanging off his belt. Subtle but obvious. 'Absolutely', I reply, 'not a problem, straight away'. No more convincing required, thanks for asking!

That's the thing in America, guns everywhere. One time we were at a restaurant in Arizona and there was a sign at the door stating, 'Please leave your guns outside'. We thought it was a joke sign, but it was serious!

The workers at Cal Neva were so generous, good fun and we shared the culture liberally. (The university would have been proud, mission successful.) One work colleague owned a Mustang and would take us for spins through the mountains to Reno. Wow. They kept offering us cocaine, but I always resisted, scared I'd get addicted because it was so readily available. They described the effect it has on them, made them feel bulletproof and on top of the world. 'It melts away our problems.' I'm thinking life is so good without, why take the risk?

To snort or not snort? There are lines I won't cross.

Cal Neva and the general area were really buzzing at the time we were there. Frank Sinatra's Show Room was in full swing with great musicals. Sometimes the waitresses would get a US$100 tip for just delivering a meal or a drink to a rich customer. There were plenty of rich customers. In 1982 $US100 was a lot of cash to a university student.

I have since been back twice over the years. Each time I noticed a degradation in the operation of the resort. It was very sad to see, what was once an iconic and famous venue, deteriorate into a mess. I now (2024) notice on Google maps that it has closed altogether and is fenced off. What a shame, all this lost history. A Google search shows the new owner is renovating it, with the intention for the opening to occur in 2026 to align with the 100-year celebrations since the original opening of Cal Neva. Might be worth a visit if it really happens?

Before and after the time at Cal Neva I had the opportunity to travel to both the East and West coasts of the States. The national parks are breathtaking, and the museums at Washington DC are amazing.

There are five of us in the gigantic old Cadillac. It has been loaned to us by a friend of one of the girls in our Australian group. Their instruction is to abandon the car when we are finished travelling; it isn't worth retrieving. It has a big gash down one side from when a snow plough opened it up whilst clearing a one-meter high snow drift from the car park at Cal Neva casino. Such is life.

We pass through Yosemite National Park. The snow is melting in the Sierra Nevada mountains and the waterfalls are tremendous, powering over the 4,000-foot granite cliffs that dominate the park and that rise straight up all around us. The sun is sparkling off the water droplets as they cascade down the rocks. It is captivating. I can feel the energy.

We make it to the edge of the Grand Canyon in the old car. It is just after winter, and the snow still peppers the tops of the canyon walls. The vastness of the canyon below is beckoning. We decide to go for a short walk down from the top where we are parked, maybe just an hour down and back to soak up the setting. The call of the Canyon is overpowering.

The walk is as captivating as it is addictive. The scenery is breathtaking. We keep walking down, down, down. The geology keeps changing as we continue. No-one suggests it is time to return to the car. We are mesmerised; in the moment.

In time we are closer to the bottom than the top, and we press on, very curious to explore the snaking Colorado River that formed the canyon millions of years ago. It is late afternoon when we reach the river, and we suddenly realise it is too late to return to the car. It is some 14 miles of track away and one mile vertically above us. How have we miscalculated so badly? We had only intended to be away from the car for an hour or so. Fortunately we find a hostel nearby. It is run by the First Nations people of the area, and the only option for accommodation. It is called Phantom Ranch. 'Did anyone bring any money down here?', I ask tentatively, because I know I haven't. We quickly tally up everyone's loose change and go to the reception. We just have enough for one room, an orange and some bread. It is going to be a long night; we are all starving from the exercise of the trek. There would be no breakfast the next day either.

The setting is just glorious. The canyon walls rise up for what seems forever. The river, a series of turbulent rapids. Despite the temperature at the top of the canyon being near freezing, down here is sunbaking temperature. We spot some guys fishing for trout in the river. Always one to spot an opportunity, we send over the most charismatic of our crew to investigate and hopefully return with some fish. To our amazement the girls return with a handful of trout to compliment our meagre rations. Things are getting biblical!

Fish to share amongst five – where's Jesus when we need Him?

The next morning, I try to get up and my legs won't work. The pain in the muscles is overwhelming. I guess the thud, thud of the 14-mile constant downhill trek has taken its toll.

Everyones' comments are the same. Even though we are young and fit, and had just finished months of demanding downhill skiing, we must have used different muscles in the walk down. We have a very long uphill walk ahead of us, and the sooner we start the better, as we have no food left. It takes about half an hour of painful walking to get the legs working properly again. We finally reach the car, and a takeaway joint, and eat up big.

In 2009/2010 I took my family back to that area to show them around. These days you need a permit to walk to Phantom Ranch and need to book well ahead. At the start of the walk there are all these warning signs about being prepared, take lots of food and especially water, be prepared for changes in weather, and that people have died of dehydration doing this walk, bla, bla, bla. Thankfully there were no signs when we set off in February 1982, else we may have not ventured to the bottom.

The States adventure is coming to an end. After the Grand Canyon we travel to Washington DC having a great time meeting friends and visiting fantastic museums. I am now on a stop-over in Denver airport on the way to LA to catch my Qantas flight home later tonight. The flight to LA leaves in two hours. I am called up to the check in desk. I am told, 'Mr Sockhill, your seat to LA has been cancelled because you didn't reconfirm it within the last 24 hours. It has been filled by another person'. I have no money left; in fact, I owe my friends $15.00. I am relying on airplane food to get me home, and I definitely can't afford any overnight accommodation. The receptionist kindly offers to put me on a waitlist in case someone doesn't turn up. I enquire how long the wait list is, I'm sixth on the list.

So this is a predicament; I'll probably miss my international flight home and I have no money, my last traveller's cheque is cashed in and spent! I can hear them calling the odd person up to the check in; they must be slowly going through the waitlist. Time is fast running out. I start to get very concerned (unusual). I realise what has happened; they have intentionally over booked the plane, counting on some people not arriving in time. They mis-calculated, and I'm going to be collateral damage. Time to get angry. I go up to the check in and start explaining my predicament, that I'll be stranded in America with no money and no flight home. I pound the bench in frustration, my voice raised. Before long they have found me a seat, I must have been convincing, thank God!

The working holiday to the USA catalysed my desire for travel and adventure.

A couple of years later I was on another travel odyssey. I had been working for 18 months and had saved up some money. I had a friend in Ayr in the travel business. I went to see her with a map of the world. I had put 12 crosses on the map and asked her to book me on flights that connected the dots. I spent three months taking in Japan, Hong Kong, China, Europe, USA, Egypt, Singapore and so on.

The trip gave me the perspective that travelling the world with a backpack is a very good character-building experience. This was travel before the days of the internet and mobile phones. One had to plan well ahead and use paper-back travel guides etc. to make it work. It forces one to plan properly, to think things through, to use initiative and to manage in a crisis.

An example was when I arrived at a European youth hostel at 8.00 pm one night in a very isolated location to find it was closed for winter. I had to find somewhere else to stay the night, no phone to assist, and it was cold. I paid the price for poor prior planning and had to rescue my situation. All good character-building experience. There was no one to blame but myself, full personal accountability.

On that whirl-wind trip, I landed in Cairo and had a one-week tour booked for the next morning. Only one problem, my backpack was lost in transit by the airline. I had to join the tour without it. Fortunately, I had all my travel documents and travellers' cheques (yes, cheques, no tap and go in those days) with me. So, without hesitation I went and bought a long Egyptian robe, a headpiece, a pair of sunglasses and a toothbrush. I have memorable photos of myself sitting on a camel in the traditional local fashion with the pyramids in the background. Another time I went sailing on the

Nile at Aswan in the traditional sailing vessel, known as a felucca. The Nile River at Aswan presents a very relaxing setting. The temples at Abu Simbel are awe inspiring. The original temples were to be flooded when the Aswan high dam was built, so the temples were relocated above the water line at great cost.

Walk like an Egyptian. A week in Egypt.

Fortunately, my backpack was at the airport when I went to take off for Singapore one week later. The robe and headpiece often came in handy back home. I used it as a dress up at theme parties. One such party in Brisbane was themed by the letter T. There was only one option here, I dressed up as a terrorist with fake explosives formed into an obvious suicide belt which was strapped onto me before I left for the party. I didn't think this through very well. On the way to the party, I remembered I needed to stop and get some drinks, so I pulled into a drive through and jumped out of the car.

The drive through manager saw me and did a double take, the look of terror in his eyes. 'Whooaa, you ARE going to a fancy dress party, aren't you?!' he uttered. 'All good mate, don't worry', I quickly replied, realising what I had done. Whoops!

At the party I was out the back talking to the host and another guest approached. 'The cops are out the front, and they want to speak to the owner', he said. Now, I've had experience in handling these exact situations, so asked the house owner, 'Do you want me to go and deal with this one?'. A firm NO was the response. 'Just trying to help!'.

I digress - back to the trip around the world.

The last stop was Perth. I had many friends in Perth, and it was on the path home, so why not make it a stopover? The America's Cup was on, and a good friend had scored tickets on an ocean liner to watch it close up. (Thanks Kathy) A great day out.

The night before I left Perth there was a cocktail party. It was a big night, and I had an early morning flight home. I missed the flight. I had organised my flatmates to meet me at Townsville airport as we lived an hour's drive away in Ayr. I completely forgot to tell them I had missed the flight, perhaps I wasn't fully functional that morning?

When I did finally get home a couple of days later, I was astonished to see all my worldly possessions on the footpath outside our rental accommodation. I am talking, bed, wardrobe, tables, clothes, absolutely everything! Apparently my flatmates were a bit pissed they went all the way to Townsville to pick me up and I was a no-show. How inconsiderate!

Hitch hiking is always an experience.

I am hitchhiking through the Italian Alps and accept a ride in a BMW sports car. Seems like a cool idea at the time. Off we go at breakneck speed along the mountain curves. It gets hairy. The driver is now overtaking on double lines, the whole works. It's quickly becoming very scary. After a while I start to analyse what is really going on. The driver is signalling to the cars in front before he overtakes on a very blind tight bend. The car in front signals back, they both understand, and as we pass, the other car moves over to make safe room. Everyone is on the same page. Once I realise the full situation, I settle back and enjoy the ride. It's all a matter of understanding the context. Take the risk!

I have hitchhiked in many places around the world, and only knocked back one lift. It was in Australia, near Mount Gambier. The day started off nice enough, so I set off with the thumb out. I got a lift, but they had to drop me off miles from nowhere, as they had to turn off to another place. The weather was deteriorating and there wasn't much traffic. Then a storm came through and it started to rain, very cold. Just as I thought it couldn't get any worse the hail started. A car pulled up to offer me a lift and I looked inside to assess the situation. The car was an old bomb, and filthy. The dog on the back seat didn't look very friendly. The two people in the car looked very feral, and this is before 'feral' was a word used to describe humans. It just looked like a scary proposition. I stepped back, thanked them for stopping, but said I was enjoying the walk?! Bring on the hail!

A few years after the Tahoe experience, I got a call from one of the guys who was in Tahoe with me. He was a character, and we really got on well. He invited me on an organised trip to Europe for snow skiing. His good friend owned a travel company, and everything was organised. There were about 12 in the group and the plan was to land in Paris, buy three Citroens, spend one week in each of four European ski resorts (Italian Dolomites, Les Arcs in France and two Austrian resorts), return to Paris and sell the Citroens back at a pre-arranged price. He mentioned that he knew several of the others and they were all good fun. Coming from this guy, the word 'fun' inspired my imagination.

We picked the three cars up from a dealership that was located near the Arc De Triomphe. First up was a couple of laps. For those who haven't been there the circle road around the Arc De Triomphe is 8 lanes but there are no line markings. Total chaos, but good fun. That done we headed off into the country.

What could possibly go wrong?

The first car problem occurred when they (I was in one of the other cars) filled the Citroen with the wrong fuel and blew the engine up. The car was a write off.

The second incident occurred when one of the guys went out night clubbing at a neighbouring resort. He was driving home and went over a very steep embankment, rolling the car several times before coming to rest against some trees. It was 2.00 am in the morning. He managed to get out of the car and crawl back up to the road, then get assistance. He was lucky he wasn't killed with hypothermia. The Citroen was a write off. As Meatloaf would say, '2 outta 3 ain't bad', except...

One Citroen left; the car I was in. We went up to the pub for dinner. Coming back the driver must have been a bit too relaxed and was on the wrong side of the road (stupid European road rules). A head on collision resulted, luckily at low speed and no-one was hurt. The Citroen was a write off. The police turned up, but we couldn't understand a word. He was waving his arms around furiously.

Fortunately, we had full insurance and continued our trip with a rental car. Such is life.

Later in the holiday we travelled to a neighbouring resort for the weekend to see friends at a skiing competition. We arrived in our car late at night with practically no fuel in the tank, and everything was closed for the night. We had planned to couch surf with our friends but couldn't find them; they were out, and their accommodation was locked. It was a fairly loose arrangement. We had no option but to sleep in the car, in well below freezing conditions. I never realised being cold could be so painful. Lesson learnt...the hard way.

I particularly remember Les Arc Ski Resort in Chamonix region France.

The weather is perfect. It is my last day at this resort and fine powder snow carpets the slopes. The mountains stretch out before us, as far as the eye can see. I have booked a hang-gliding experience through the French Alps, and I am so looking forward to it, despite not really being sure what to expect.

I make my way to the allotted area and meet my guide. He explains everything to me. I am harnessed to him and stand in front. With skis on we both start skiing down the long ski run in front of us. As the mountain drops off in steepness, we gain speed. Before long we are flying through the thin cold mountain air. The take-off is so smooth and easy. We then start soaring around the alps, taking in the scenery. No noise except for the swish of the breeze. Rushing past cliffs and over ridges. Flying with the birds. After some time, my guide finds another long slope and we glide down for a smooth touch down. What an experience, and I live to tell the story.

Despite the car issues it is a fantastic holiday. The skiing and the resorts are first class.

It is 2009 and I am back in the USA with my family, showing them around some of the areas I visited when I was young and carefree. They get the edited version. We have just visited the Hoover Dam on the Colorado river, a short drive from Las Vegas. It was built during the great depression to stimulate employment. I cannot believe the change within Las Vegas from my 1982 trip. A completely new casino strip. Amazing. I can never forget a classic one liner from Las Vegas. I am in the information centre starting to ask a question, 'Is it possible...'. I am cut off mid-sentence, 'ANYTHING IS POSSIBLE IN LAS VEGAS', in this loud voice with a strong accent. So funny, and probably true.

It is early afternoon, and we are now on the interstate to the Grand Canyon. It's about 450 km away and should be a 5-hour drive. Our accommodation is booked near the entrance track to Phantom Ranch, the place I walked to in 1982. The drive is slowly uphill, all the way. The Grand Canyon is one mile deep. Unknown to us there has recently been huge snowstorms in the area. The roads are now all iced up ahead where the terrain is higher. The traffic grinds to a halt, we still don't realise why, but it's not moving. We slowly move on and pass an exit road. We see the trucks spinning their wheels on the steep exit road, they are going nowhere. It then dawns on us what is happening, the snow has turned to ice and the trucks are blocking all the exits.

There is no way out, we are effectively blocked in. I check the fuel tank and ask my wife what water and food we have in the car. This could take a while, and it is literally freezing outside. Four hours later and I estimate we have moved about ten miles. It is now dark outside, and the temperature has dropped. Thank God I refuelled in Las Vegas, and I can keep the engine running to stay warm. The three kids in the back are getting agitated. The girls (my wife and daughter) want to pee but there are no normal options here on the road. Finally, they can't wait any longer and have to go beside the car. The line of trucks behind us understands what is happening and they turn their headlights off. How considerate!

At one am I spot an exit where the line of trucks is actually moving, ever so slowly. I take the exit, and, as if by some miracle, I find a vacant room in a hotel. My wife cooks some instant noodles for dinner; it's now 1.30 in the morning.

When I wake up, the hire car has a flat tyre. What else can go wrong?

It's not long before the traffic is moving again, and we resume our travels towards the Grand Canyon. We arrive at our hotel a day late, and it is a beautiful sunny day, not one cloud. I see a sign saying helicopter flights over the Canyon and cannot resist the temptation. What a contrast to the turmoil of yesterday, as we fly over the canyon and down to the Colorado river at the bottom. I am trying to spot the track where I walked in 1982. What a place. The helicopter experience just reinforces how big this landscape really is. Just breathtaking.

We left the Canyon and ventured on to Lake Tahoe via Yosemite for a week of snow skiing at Squaw Valley, my old stamping ground. KT 22 awaits my return. I had more tales to tell my family!

During my working career as a manager, I would always ask prospective employees at interviews what travel experiences they have had. I would give extra marks to those who had travelled alone internationally with just a backpack and a frugal budget.

From my experience travel inspires and reinforces several great attributes.

- It develops a can-do attitude.
- It teaches self-accountability.
- It rewards initiative and risk taking and provides lessons from failures.
- It shows the value in planning ahead.
- It develops confidence in relationship building.
- It develops a flexible, creative and adaptive approach.

Chapter 13

Cyprus

My wife, Ann, has Cypriot ancestry. Her father was born in Cyprus as were her mothers' parents. We have been there on three occasions to visit her relatives. Each time has been a fascinating experience. The relatives show us around everywhere and explain the culture and history. Cyprus is very centrally located in the Mediterranean. Over the centuries it has always been a very sought-after location and for this reason it has been taken over several times by different forces. In 1974 Turkey invaded Cyprus. The country is still divided as a result. The northern third is occupied by the Turkish people. It is divided by a no-go green line patrolled by the United Nations. There are still areas close to the green line that are unoccupied. My wife has relatives who had to move away from home the night of the invasion and have never been allowed to return. They were told to pack for three days max.

It is 2019. We are staying in the capital, Nicosia. Over breakfast our host (my wife's cousin) casually asks if I heard the explosion last night. 'No, what do you mean?', I ask. The reply scares me. 'Last night an out-of-control missile from the middle east crashed in the hills 20 km north of here. The explosion was heard up to 60 km away. Don't worry, they are saying it was a one-off thing!'.

Yeah right.

We are now driving around Nicosia. It is a mixture of very old stone buildings and new developments. The roads are mostly not good, and progress is slow. The traffic is busy. Up ahead the road is sandbagged and blocked off. The buildings above the sandbags look deserted and derelict. We turn the corner and continue down a side street. 'What's going on back there?', I ask Ann's cousin, 'With the roadblock and the sandbags?'.

'That's the border to the Turkish occupied area', comes the response and I learn all about the long night of the invasion. Animosity is still very thick.

Looking at the Cypriot no-go zone towards the Turkish occupied territory.

The current concern (2019) is that the Turks are drilling for oil in the waters off Cyprus, in the Cyprus economic zone. There is always a conflict or a threat going on in Cyprus.

We leave Nicosia and are travelling south to visit the village where my father-in-law was born. First we pass through the little villages on the road up to Mount Troodos right in the middle of Cyprus. On top of Mt Troodos there is a military zone for the UK. At over 6,000 feet high, the UK can keep an eye on the Middle East, which is only about 250 km to the east.

We stop at the villages, buy some fresh bread from the street markets and get more history lessons.

We have lunch at a mountain village restaurant. Food is always a big deal in Cyprus. It is not a rushed event. Meze is the norm. It is an ongoing procession of different dishes, often finger food. Plate after plate. One never knows when it is finished. Olives, halloumi (cheese), dolmades (lemon rice in grapevine leaves), keftethes (meatballs), octopus, calamari, home-made sausage, salada (Greek salad), lamb souvlaki, fish. At one meal I thought it was done, until the host grabbed half a chicken and dumped it on my plate with the advice, 'In Cyprus we eat'! Not a question about if I was still hungry. At the mountain village restaurant we drink the home-made red wine from the house down the street. It is so nice that I ask if I can buy some to take away. They say sorry, the guy who makes it is away for the day. Towards the end of the meal, they bring me a multi-purpose four litre plastic container of the home-made wine. 'We found the person who made it, they returned home, here is your wine!'.

Over lunch I learn about 'the haircut'. Everyone is still really angry about the haircut, despite it happening about 6 years previously in 2013. Every household bank account with over 100,000 euros lost 47% of their account holdings over 100,000 euros, no questions asked. They woke up one morning and it was removed from their bank accounts overnight. The reason given was that the government needed the money more than the people did. This is how Cyprus managed the financial crisis. If you had happened to empty your bank account the day before by buying say, a restaurant, you were not affected!

We move on to explore Armou, my father-in-law's village high up in the hills above Paphos, in southern Cyprus. The best description I can muster is that it is simply biblical and lost in time. Every building is very old, made of stone. The streets are narrow, some with cobblestones. They wind around tight corners in a seemingly random way. The buildings come right out to the street, no footpaths, no front yards. There are no shops, no hotels, no accommodation houses, and only one church.

Ann at her Dad's home in Cyprus.

I can't see many people anywhere. There are small orange orchards and olive groves mixed in randomly with the houses. To the west, in the distance, the Mediterranean sparkles in the sunshine.

I look for the donkeys, as they are a treasured animal in these parts.

We find the actual house where my father-in-law was born and lived in as a child. We knock on the door. It has been bought by an English couple. We are welcomed in. Some of the original cooking implements are hanging on the wall. The fourni (an oven that is built into a stone wall and fired with wood) remains intact.

It is a great and emotional insight into how the villagers lived many years ago.

It is now late afternoon, and the sun is setting through the olive groves. All shades of red, orange and pink are scattering through the clouds on the horizon, reflecting off the ocean in the distance. Hardly a sound to be heard. This village is still lost in time, so charming. An easy place in which to relax.

Despite all the issues in Cyprus, it is managing reasonably well financially, and the living quality is good, much better than I expected. Tourism is a major source of income for the country as Cyprus has a great climate relative to many other European destinations to the north.

At the time of writing (2024), Hamas is accusing Cyprus of assisting Israel in the Middle East conflict and is threatening to take action against Cyprus if they don't cease. In fact, Cyprus is providing aid by ship as they are a close neighbour by ocean.

Chapter 14

Reflections at lunch

We have had a long morning on the river, and are now looking for a nice place to stop for lunch. We are starving; it's been a long time since the early quick breakfast. A sand bank appears on the side of the river. It is a beautiful setting with weird cliffs interspersed with bright green forest that seems to grow out of the rocks. We tether the rafts safely and crack open the food barrel. We still have an assortment of cheeses, salami, crackers, some fruit cake, nuts and other nibbles. The guy who attached himself to our expedition has his usual handful of nuts and sultanas.

We discuss what an interesting morning it has been, and how great the weather is. We have passed underneath waterfalls that flow in from side streams. It is a warmer day and we find the shower from the falls very refreshing. We encounter beautiful deep rock reflections from the soaring cliffs.

Today's rapids are fairly easy but exhilarating. Long and dynamic with lots of spray in the face. Maybe a reflection of my working career, mostly stable and interesting, but quite often with some dynamic interference, sometimes too dynamic.

Work Experiences

As mentioned, my working career was delayed for lack of opportunities. I finally managed to get a job 12 months after graduating, but it was a seasonal position. And there was another catch. I had to venture into North Queensland country. I secured a job in a sugar mill west of Mackay right up the end of the Pioneer Valley, close to the edge of the earth. Cattle Creek Mill was a step back in time. It was located at Finch Hatton, a one pub town in the country. I knew no one in the area.

I was the first university graduate to have ever worked in the mill. In hindsight I probably jumped into the deep end with this experience, but I didn't realise this at the time. My job was as a shift chemist, so I was responsible for the operation of the chemistry part of the sugar mill. The other half of the factory was managed by a shift engineer who was responsible for the engineering aspects. So together we managed the operation of the factory overnight. The buck stopped with us. Traditionally a shift chemist would take several years of specific training to reach that goal. I was new in town, with a degree, and thrown into the job with only 2 weeks training. I was seen with intrigue, unhealthy scepticism and suspicion amongst many of the workers at the factory. In addition to this, there was a strong traditional rift between the engineers and the chemists. This was typical in the sugar industry at the time, and I didn't really understand this. As a fresh innocent face, I naturally assumed you should really try to understand and work well with your shift co-manager to optimize the whole factory. Hence I worked well with, and respected the engineers. This unfortunately put me right out of favour with all the chemists. So, this work experience ended up being a character-building experience, which taught me a lot about the value of relationships. It became a good learning experience.

Due to my very limited training in what was a complex factory, I was very reliant on the operators reporting to me. This also developed my relationship-building skills. Some of the operators were 'alcoholics' and turned up to start the shift very drunk. This added to the challenge. This situation would just not be accepted today, but back then it was let slide by senior management. I don't remember any policies around this and workplace health and safety was at a low ebb back then.

The following year I took my first permanent job at Inkerman Sugar Mill in Home Hill. I arrived in Home Hill with all my worldly possessions (including snow skis, as of course you would going to NQ), in and on top of my hand painted, water injected HQ Holden. It had several after-market modifications like a power aerial and air conditioner. Its best feature was a solid rubber mat under my feet to cover up some corrosion holes in the floor. I was tired of my feet getting wet from road water splashing up through the floor when driving in the rain. More on this iconic car later!

My main task at the mill was to computerise a large section of the factory. The mill was very backward in this regard, and everything was manually controlled with operators turning hand valves. Automation during this period was seen by unions as code for potentially eliminating jobs. Sugar mills are strongly militant workplaces. Back then unions were much stronger than today, and there was effective coercive compulsory unionism.

As an example, I was in the manager's office one day (1984) having a meeting with him when the union organiser dropped in and asked to see the manager; just a quick question. The manager agreed to a chat then and there, so I sat on the sideline and listened. The union organiser asked for something the manager could not immediately agree to. The union guy politely asked if he could use the manager's phone to make an unspecified arrangement. The manager agreed. The union organiser rang up the mill control room, which was crushing along well at the time and instructed, 'Pull her up boys!'. He had stopped operations right there and then in front of the manager, courtesy of using the manager's phone. Today that would be seen as illegal activity. This proved to be a real learning experience for me that I would lean on later in my management role at a neighbouring sugar mill.

That same union organiser was the overhead crane operator. He had a union-negotiated workplace agreement where he was the only person allowed to operate that crane. Consequently, he received all the overtime payments associated with the use of that crane after business hours, a quite substantial gain for him. Again today, that type of arrangement is totally unheard of.

One month into my new job at Inkerman Mill the manager and the industrial manager walked into my office. This was unusual, I was intrigued. Opening statement, 'Doug, don't be concerned, we'll handle it, but it looks like the workers are going on strike over what you did on the weekend when you were in here at work!'.

'Oh umm, what did I do wrong?' I asked incongruously, a look of total confusion on my face. 'They are saying you used your computer to start up a sugar mixer in the factory, and they are not happy', came the reply.

So, this shows how strong the union influence was back then. Fortunately, I could demonstrate how it was not technically possible to do what I was accused of, and the issue dissolved. Again, in today's world, there would not have been any issue if indeed I had done that.

Despite having to step around union influence, that job at Inkerman was one of my most rewarding and satisfying roles in my work career. It involved finding out from the operators every minute adjustment they did manually to control the factory, duplicating it with computer code, running simulators and then commissioning the program in the real world. This was from a base of me knowing very little of the operation to fully automating it, so it was a big step. The workdays passed quickly as I was totally immersed in the job.

CSR bought out Inkerman Mill which was part of Pioneer Sugar mills. I survived the transition and quickly progressed through technical and management roles at CSR. (I found out much later that the Inkerman Mill manager had put in a good word for me to the senior CSR Managers during the transition to CSR ownership. Quite a few of the Pioneer managers at the time did not survive the transition.)

For 12 months in 1988, I had a great opportunity at work. CSR was investigating a new way of purifying sugar juice, which was revolutionary for the world at that time. It involved using membrane filtration technology which was in its infancy. This technology could potentially greatly improve the sugar refining industry, but it wasn't straight forward. I spent weeks collecting and analysing samples of purified juice from the membrane filters.

Then I started to think creatively. This clarified cane juice could be a commercial drink product. I knew freshly squeezed cane juice was a product that was popular in SE Asia. A simple two roller mill, (not unlike Ma's washing machine ringer, except more robust) would simply squash the cane stalks and the fresh juice would be extracted. It is often sold roadside in SE Asia. (I saw these everywhere in Pakistan when I worked there in 2024.) I had actually tried this product at a market stall in Australia. Not bad.

So I started bringing the work juice samples home, trying different concentrations, adding lime juice, ginger or lemon juice etc. etc. This was not part of my job description, but what the heck.

Then I had another revelation. World Expo was coming up in Brisbane in the second half of 1988. (It became a major event in the history of Australia and ran for 6 months with over 15 million visitors.) The sugar industry was in the middle of a mega advertising campaign advertising sugar as "A NATURAL PART OF LIFE" in an attempt to offset a lot of bad publicity from marketing sources in an increasingly health-conscious society. Artificial sweeteners were also a real threat.

I could take freshly squeezed cane juice to Brisbane World Expo as a personal entrepreneurial business. I quickly realised I had everything I needed to do this, without any input from CSR.

I knew cane farmers just south of Brisbane who could supply me the cane. Tick.

I had friends in Brisbane who could manage and run the venture. Tick.

I had found a small two roller crushing mill to turn cane stalks into juice. Tick.

All I needed was a small space within the World Expo precinct to set up the stall. After many unsuccessful attempts I finally came to the realisation that no more store sites were available, I had left it too late. Annoying.

Soon after realising this, I was in CSR Sugar Mills Brisbane head office at meetings. I was talking to the mills group head of technology after one of the meetings, and casually mentioned my idea to him, explaining I could not get a store location. The guy I mentioned this to loved new ideas and was also creative. He asked me a bunch of questions then took me into the office of the mills group General Manager and explained everything to him. (The mills group General Manager was considered a God like person to young engineers in those days.) We came up with a plan to take the concept to the Queensland Sugar Board (QSB). This was the peak lobby and control group for the sugar industry at the time. They were actually running a large exhibit at World Expo and had the space to do whatever they wanted. Our idea was to offer the freshly squeezed cane juice to (the 15 million) customers as they filed past in the inevitable long queues that defined the world expo. Now that's what I call a captive market! The QSB theme was also 'Sugar is a natural part of life'. Intrinsically perfect! Or so we thought. CSR was the biggest player in the sugar industry and had a lot of clout with the QSB. I was confident this was it.

Unbelievably word came back soon after from the QSB that their marketing regime was set and fixed, and they didn't want to interfere with it. Damn! Back to North Queensland and reality. If this had gone ahead, it would have led to an incredibly exciting set of rapids in my life. Who knows where my life would have veered to after Expo had finished?

Together with CSR technologists and engineers we designed, constructed and commissioned revolutionary new equipment (continuous vacuum pans) for the CSR sugar mills. Up until then CSR had only used batch pans. Continuous pans offered several advantages as they were cheaper and took up less room which is a big advantage when sugar mills expand production.

During this part of my career I was the production manager of the largest sugar mill in Australia; it was effectively the size of two average factories. This made it a very complicated factory to operate and made my job very busy. There were always many issues going on. I constantly had a line of people at my office door asking for solutions to their (our) problems. We usually managed to work out everything together and resolve the issues by the end of each day. Despite this my manager called me in and told me I had to work more hours. I was already working ten hour days or more, and also working on weekends as the factory runs 24/7. I politely told him that I will continue to work until all problems are resolved but I won't stay back for no real reason. This was how I had been operating up until then and I thought it was working fine. I told him I had a family to get home to and they were also a priority, and that I did not think I was turning my back on work issues. I also said for him to be sure to let me know where I was underperforming. I suspect that because he was a work-a-holic he expected me to be one as well.

Not too long after I was transferred to a smaller mill, an effective demotion. At the time I was not impressed but it turned out to be a good career move in the longer term as more promotions followed, against the normal flow.

I think this goes to show sometimes you think you have been dealt an unfair play, but things work out. I ponder how the Franklin can sometimes play this situation on you. For example you find yourself in a difficult and unexpected rapid and deal with it successfully. You come out at the end of the rapid feeling a sense of achievement and success.

One particular highlight was venturing to Brazil in 2012 to investigate sugar mill equipment that was not used in Australia. I had some good introductions into the Brazil sugar industry as I had shown some Brazilians around the mill where I worked, and they were keen to reciprocate. We spent a week travelling throughout the country by car and helicopter, looking into how they utilised this equipment. CSR bought into the new technology on my return with my recommendation. We commissioned and fine-tuned the new equipment with success. It was a very rewarding experience. The new equipment solved a particularly problematic issue that was plaguing the factory where I worked for decades. It needed a good look outside of the box to solve. The Sugar Research Institute provided integral assistance in the process.

Travelling around the Brazilian sugar industry was an enlightening experience. I was amazed at how large and financially successful it had become. More on this later.

The unions continued to flex their muscles as time went on. Every two to three years all the CSR mills would have enterprise bargaining agreements re-negotiated. These were difficult negotiations. I was Production Manager at Kalamia Sugar Mill during one of these. Agreement could not be reached so all employees at all CSR mills (7 at the time) went on strike. Group management decided to lock out all employees as a return volley. All hell broke loose; this had never been done before. The employees still turned up to work each day (without pay) and formed on-site protests.

At Kalamia, they set up their protest on the edge of the factory close to our management office. Soon a band (yes, a musical band with drums, electric guitars etc.) started playing each day; loud. They had the BBQ going as well. I guess they were finding ways to not get bored sitting around all day doing nothing. Management took the position not to get them evicted, so they just hung around. This went on for several days whilst negotiations were stalled. Finally, they went next level and stormed our office. So I am talking, over one hundred angry mill workers marching over and rattling our doors and windows, and yelling 'advice!'. We as staff were all locked inside the building until they ran out of puff. Happy days.

The most dramatic day of my work experience was not easy. I was managing a mill and was informed that the main union rep had stolen building materials from work and that he had taken them home. I was shown pictures and there was no doubt about it. This was going to be a tough situation because of the strength of the unions as previously discussed.

As site manager I had to go around to his house and talk it through. He ended up taking the option to resign; he had little choice. This all went surprisingly smoothly, until his assistant union rep, Gary, quickly found out and went into the factory (which was operating at the time) on his day off. Gary went into the factory control room and stopped all operations (déjà vu all over again from Inkerman Mill, 1984). He claimed he was going to organise an impromptu union meeting to discuss the issue of his union boss resigning. He was calling it 'effective constructive dismissal'. This would mean the factory would have to be totally shut down and restarted which would cost hundreds of thousands of dollars. To be legal, stop work meetings need to be organised in advance with fair warning given to the company.

I went to the control room to discuss how this was not appropriate. These were serious rapids that required careful navigation.

Gary had already told the operators to stop the crushing mills, the first step in a total shut down, which takes many hours to take effect. This confronted me with a very difficult situation. What would I do if he would not reverse his actions? It is a major step to summarily dismiss an employee; it is hardly ever done and for good reason. There are very few circumstances that allow it to happen. This person's livelihood rested on the decision I was about to make. To say I was feeling anxious was a major understatement!

I had quite a good relationship with Gary. He's a good bloke who you could have a bit of a yarn with. I was now concerned that this relationship was about to fly out the window and be lost.

I approach the control room and tentatively open the door. I see many faces inside, many more than normal. Gary is talking with the operators and turns to look at me when I enter. 'Gary what's going on? I am told the mills have been stopped.' Gary comes over and his piercing blue eyes lock onto mine. 'I have had to pull her up, Doug. I am organising a union meeting and need everyone to attend. The only way to do this is to stop crushing so everyone can leave their workplace and gather with me for the meeting.'

'Is that really necessary? It'll take hours to stop properly. Can't we talk about this?' I am finding it difficult to believe this is actually happening. 'No Doug, we have to do this. We have a lot to discuss, and everyone needs to have a say.' Gary's eyes are staring straight through me. I can see for sure that this is not going to end well. He has definitely made up his mind. I know I have to give him ample opportunity so I go through a process to give him time to reconsider.

'Gary, it is really important that you understand what I am about to tell you, and that you think about it and your actions very carefully. What you are doing here is illegal, as you haven't given the company the required notice period for this strike action. If you don't allow crushing to restart, I will have to terminate your employment, and I don't want to go down that path. You will leave me no option.'

'Not happening Doug, we're all organised to have the meeting',

I can just see that he is set in his mind. I have not seen this look in his eyes before.

And so it went on, I gave Gary a clear three opportunities to allow operations to resume. I had to take the horrible decision to dismiss Gary. Unfortunately there are never any winners in these situations.

That night the story was all over the television news. It took a while to blow over with the district union office getting involved with senior mills group management to smooth out the situation. The unions were not happy, it was unprecedented that two union representatives were dismissed in one day.

I was at junior touch football with my children a couple of months later and I saw Gary walking toward me. This was worrying, as I thought for sure he'd still be holding animosity towards me. To his credit he extended a hand and said, 'Doug I just wanted to say you were right what you did to me. I was out of line'. Wow. You could have knocked me over with a feather! All credit to the man. As I said, he was a good bloke. This was a tough life experience. This goes to show how strong the union was. Gary had put union affiliation and loyalty ahead of his job. A big call.

As I write this section (2024), I read that the workers at the mills where I worked are on strike again. It is EBA negotiation time, and the unions have strategically delayed negotiations to when the crushing season is about to start. This is when they have maximum negotiating strength. Deja vu all over again!

The final mill I worked at was Pioneer Mill, also near Ayr. By this time a Singaporean company called Wilmar had purchased CSR sugar mills. Pioneer was a particularly interesting mill to work at because it also generated 50 MW into the electricity grid. This is very unusual for Australian mills and completely changes how you need to optimise the operation of the factory because energy conservation goes to a completely higher level of focus. I had some very bright engineers working for me to assist in the fine tuning of operations. I found it very rewarding working in a more technically complicated and demanding work environment. We had a great team.

In time senior mills group management completely changed the working structure in the mills, which in my view was a backward step. The new structure broke down existing good working relationships and getting work completed became unnecessarily complicated. People who spoke up soon regretted speaking up. They also reduced the site-based authority with centralised policies. My day was getting filled up with repetitive report writing and meetings, instead of making practical improvements. The challenge of successfully operating a sugar mill is difficult enough as it is, without all these time wasters.

I made a principled decision to retire early. This was a big and unusual call at the time. It was difficult to leave the great team that worked for me. They were bright and supportive. I disagreed with the new arrangements and the (sometimes toxic) management style that came with them. I had lost respect for the company that historically earned and deserved much respect from myself and my work colleagues. So many of my friends and colleagues at work felt the same way as myself, but they were not financially secure enough to leave. I felt for them.

When you work at the sugar mills, it becomes your life.

You live in a work supplied house in a work housing estate.

Your kids form friendships with the kids of your work colleagues.

Your kids settle into a school with the other kids on the estate.

Partners form strong friendships with the other partners on the estate.

You probably don't own a house because you haven't needed to. Work becomes your life. Life becomes entrenched, and difficult to leave.

I recognised this early on and took measures to ensure I had a plan B ready to go. I had managed it so I could leave, easily, at any time, and I did.

Interestingly, six years after I left, a new Australian chief executive came in and basically reversed many of the structural changes that I had disagreed with, and demoted some of the managers that I thought should have been demoted. It's called karma.

During my working career as a mill Manager, I had the responsibility to interact closely with the cane growers. The meetings were always interesting, and I made some good relationships with some of the canegrower's leadership who were involved in these meetings. The meetings were not always easy, as there were often conflicting goals, but we normally managed to work things through.

I had often heard stories and rumours about life in the cane fields in the 1930's and 1940's. Stories about the mafia allegedly having control of the cane growers, especially north of Townsville. The word was, if you found a white feather in your letter box, watch out! This meant you had crossed the line with the unwritten rules of those in silent control and trouble was close by. There were stories of people getting kneecapped (hit with a baseball bat) and about houses getting burnt down. Cane fields would get burnt before the mill started crushing which results in no income for the year for the grower concerned. I never really knew if the stories were true, but they were rife. Some were even told to me by my Italian cane growing friends.

About three years after I retired, an intriguing series called "The Black Hand" was aired on the Australian Broadcasting Corporation (ABC). It was all about the rumours I was hearing. The series also talked about the movement to Griffith of these controlling forces. I had worked in both areas! If you include my work in the Lake Tahoe area, that makes three (alleged) loose connections with the Mafia in my working career!

I spent six years managing sugar mills in the Herbert region north of Townsville. Some years after I left this region, I was working on a CSR Mills Group project to improve the interface between the cane harvesters and the CSR mills. It was a big project and about six of us from CSR went to all the Queensland mills, studied how they harvested cane, and filtered the best initiatives from every district. We wrote a report that showed how both the millers and the growers could save money from these shared learnings. I was charged with going to the Herbert Canegrowers and showing them the results, with hopefully gaining their approval to introduce the changes to the advantage of all concerned.

There was always a low trust level generally between the growers and CSR. I knew this but thought the dollar savings would still be good enough to garner some interest. Also, I knew these guys well from managing the mills there for six years. I knew they were a fairly hard-hitting, direct talking bunch of guys, but we did have some level of respect for each other. We had sorted out issues by working together in the past. Still, with some trepidation, my colleague and I entered the canegrowers board room and sat down in front of their entire board of directors. Their manager started the dictaphone without asking permission, I had never had this happen before, but ok. We delivered our report without any questions being asked, quiet as church mouses, very polite. That worried me. At the end of the meeting, we received a lecture of how their harvester operators were the best in the world and couldn't possibly improve further. Ok, were you not listening? Then I asked where we could go from here to maybe explore further possibilities together. I'll never forget the response, 'Doug do you remember how to get home, or do you want us to draw you a map?'. OK, well, I guess we'll leave now! I was gobsmacked!

This was exactly the stopper you don't want to get caught in!

Three years before I retired, I was asked to be the chair of the board for the Staff Officers Association. This is effectively the union for staff. It also covered workers at all CSR divisions (in the building industry) and Rinker (which bought out part of the CSR divisions previously). It was a part time job and involved quarterly board meetings in Sydney. I found this role very interesting and challenging. The staff association deals with unfair treatment of staff, and also aims to maintain fair working arrangements for all members. I got to see how other companies manage their workforces - the good, the bad and the ugly. I got to see the intricacies of how HR departments work, or should I say, cause disruption.

Retiring early gave me the opportunity to move to the Sunshine Coast and do some part time consultancy work, some of which enabled me to keep in touch with the global sugar industry, whilst enjoying more leisure time and travel. It wasn't until I retired that I realised how intense my job was. My retired colleagues say the same to me regularly.

Chapter 15

Yachting Days (from what I can remember)

I often wonder what would get my adrenalin flowing fastest; out at sea in a 40 knot squall in my yacht, or rafting down a wild rapid out of control, bouncing off the rocks?

We see the fog in the distance, in the direction we are heading. It hangs still, close to the horizon, stretching from the east to the west in a distinct line. Normally the fog would lift by early morning, but it is now mid-morning, and it's still clearly visible. It must have something to do with a temperature inversion, or the meeting of a cold front with warm air. We are heading to the Percy Islands, which are legendary to the yachties that ply the coast. We had been trying to stop over at Middle Percy Island a few times as we had heard all the stories about how nice it is. But to stay there the wind needs to be from a particular direction so that a parked yacht has protection by the island from the ocean swells. Now everything is right, and we are on our way. As we come to within a couple of kilometres the fog starts to surround our yacht. Lightly at first then thicker and thicker.

But before we arrive at Middle Percy, a pod of dolphins wants to put on a show for us. We are cutting through the water nicely at about six knots when a fin breaks the surface, right beside the yacht. Then another and another. I go up to the bow for a closer look. They are breaking the surface within centimetres of the bow, surfing the bow wave. Their agility is phenomenal! Never once do they hit the bow, but so close. They surf the bow wave for ages, then disappear as quickly as they had arrived.

The fog surrounds us as we sail into one of the Bays at Percy Islands.

The visibility is now down to about 50 meters. Our phone apps are switched on to show us the water depth, where the islands are and where other boats are. I don't know how sailors managed safely before satellites. Our apps tell us we are now very close to the anchorage, so we slow right down. The wind has dropped right off, I can feel the moisture sticking to my skin. As we venture slowly towards the beach, parked yachts are appearing out of the fog. The word 'weird' hardly describes the scene, it is like something out of a thriller movie where you are waiting for something to happen, but don't quite know what it is. We drop anchor and slowly the fog lifts. It is after midday and the sun is finally heating the cool moist air. Before our eyes the island starts to appear, at first the pure white sand, then the palm trees and finally the hills in the background. About 20 yachts are revealed as the fog disappears. Middle Percy has a small dwelling on the beach where the yachties gather. That night the stories start around the fire and continue as the sun sets over the water. The rums get stronger. The stories of people drifting through life metaphorically and literally. The stories of people who hitch rides from boat to boat and sleep on the beach when not sailing. The stories of people with no money, but who catch and barter fish to exist. The stories of spear fisherman who fend off sharks whilst trying to catch a meal. Tomorrow is another day. Tomorrow can wait.

Yachties' beach at Middle Percy Island. Magical place where all the good stories get told.

The weather is holding well, so after a couple of nights, we push on to Lady Musgrave Island; another iconic place of mention in all the yachting books. Another place not to miss. Lady Musgrave is more of a donut shaped coral reef with an island attached to one part. It is a couple of kilometres across and inside the ring of reef are many coral formations. There is only one way inside the reef formation, and that is through a 15-meter-wide gap in the coral. Entry can only be safe in daylight hours at high tide, as the current rips in and out at other times. Again, we had been trying to get inside Lady Musgrave for years, and now the timing is right.

We are not disappointed. The entrance channel is very narrow and tricky but so interesting as we can easily see all the corals through the crystal-clear water. It is so narrow we can check the accuracy of the GPS app on the way through. We spend the rest of the day snorkelling through the beautiful coral bommies surrounded by the immense fish life.

Glorious sunset at Lady Musgrave Island Reef

It's late in the afternoon and we see it is going to be a good sunset. The clouds are forming on the horizon. We have seen literally 100's of magnificent sunsets and sunrises from our yacht, but none like this afternoon inside Lady Musgrave reef.

For over two hours we watch the colours and intensities continually changing as the sun dances with the moving clouds on the horizon. The gin and tonics slide down easily.

Just a few stories from life on a boat...

I started yachting in Moreton bay while at Churchie (high school). My uncle (Bill, the surgeon) would take me out each week and we'd enter the yacht races. I really enjoyed the thrill of the start, and it also got me out of boarding school for the day, an extra big plus.

"Wake up Whitehaven Bay!" – with the Go-Go's playing at volume 10 – Yee-Haaa!!

When I moved north for work, I started renting yachts around the Whitsundays. On one trip, like a well-trained engineer, I did a lot of prior planning. I organised extra speakers for the deck of the (Whitsunday Rent-a-Yacht) rental yacht (these were boxed speakers from the HQ) and a cocktail blender. This was powered by a Morris minor starter motor, kindly made by a good engineering friend of mine (let's call him Ed the Engineer) on request (no 240 volts on yachts back then). I remember cruising into iconic Whitehaven Bay, stereo blasting with The Go-Go's ('we got the beat') on volume 10 through the deck mounted speakers, and the girls using the mast to pole dance on deck. Sundowners had started early!

Now, for context, Whitehaven beach is one of the most iconic beaches in Australia. It won the title of third best beach in Australia in 2024. It is a two kilometre stretch of brilliant white sand. The scenic hills rise up from the ocean at each end. The forest reaches right down to the beach. Crystal clear water completes the picture. It is normally very quiet and serene. Most people like it this way!

Climbing Whitsunday Peak (437 m) with Bruce, Jess, and Luke. Hamilton Island resort in background.

Most of the yachts left quickly, but not all. We soon had the jumper leads out and set up the blender to the battery. This was definitely not part of the official Whitsunday Rent a Yacht's instruction manual by any stretch of the imagination. (This was the instruction manual we were told to read carefully and follow closely at all times for our safety and well being.) Neither, for that matter, were the extra portable Realistic speakers that we had wired to the yacht's stereo system.

There was still one yacht parked nearby, so we called them over for a cocktail. Cocktails in hand, we settled in for a session and I asked our newfound neighbour, 'So what do you do for a crust mate?'. Shock horror with the reply as he quietly said with a smirk as he took in a long look at all our electrical handiwork before answering, 'My name is Burnie, I own Whitsunday Rent a Yacht'. Awkward!

There was no talking my way out of this one, so I went all in. 'Another margarita perhaps Bernie?'. Fortunately, Bernie had a sense of humour and a lust for the good times!

Pirate looking for trouble in the Whitsundays.

One morning we woke up in Cid Harbour. A P&O cruise liner had come in during the night and moored beside us. Nothing else for it but to sail around the liner popping champagne corks in its general direction and strongly advising them to leave our island sanctuary.

That morning, we headed off to Nara Inlet which is one of the top three anchorages in the Whitsundays. It is a tight inlet with fiord-like tree-lined hills on both sides. We went through the inlet and suddenly ran aground. This was before the navigational apps came out on phones. One was meant to take care with constant reading of maps and compass to stay out of trouble. Yeah right, that seems like a lot of work. The tide was ripping out and there was no way we could reverse back to deeper water. Only thing to do was light up the BBQ and cook up some bacon for brunch. While the bacon was cooking the rental yacht started leaning over more and more, as the tide receded. Before our very eyes the bacon fat started running nicely off the hot plate.

Bacon-angle: the angle of cooking bacon at which the bacon fat automatically runs off the BBQ plate.

Bacon-angle has since become a very important cooking concept that has stood the test of time. Every yacht should have a BBQ bolted onto the stern.

I had several charters, but the most dramatic and memorable by far goes like this. A group of us rented a yacht, but I was the only person on board who knew anything about yachts or boats. We moored at Long Island, and I took three of the crew into Club Crocodile Resort (no longer in existence) for the night to party; hard. At about 2.00 am it was time to get in the dinghy and go back to the yacht. We headed back out to where we left it moored at anchor and could not see it anywhere. I motored around for a while trying to work out what was going on. I was sure I knew where we had moored the yacht but it was nowhere to be seen. I was totally dumbstruck and started to sober up quickly! OMG what to do? The only option was to go back to the reception and tell them my predicament, not thinking they could help in any way, but what else was there to do?

Luckily it was a 24-hour reception, so I went up and said, trying not to slur too much, 'Ahh, not sure what to do but I've lost my yacht, it's gone.'

Without blinking the receptionist said, 'Don't worry, the Australian Navy is parked offshore. I'll call them and ask if they have seen it.' I was blown away. The reply came back over the two-way, 'Yes we've been watching them all night through our night vision glasses, they've drifted halfway over to the mainland!'. Unbelievable!

'Well ask them if they can go and wake them up, please, and tell them no one on board knows boats', still trying not to slur. (I was also aware that the infamous operations manual strongly forbade sailing at night, and for good reason.)

So, the navy went in their inflatable and knocked on the side of our yacht, woke up the crew and told them where they were. Fortunately, I had told them enough about boating for them to be able to get back to Long Island; I'm pretty certain with a bit of assistance from the Navy guys. Whilst this was in motion, I went down to the beach and found a banana lounge to lie on. I needed a rest. I woke up just around dawn to see the rental yacht coming back in. Praise to the Australian Navy. Job well done guys, and good to see my taxes being used effectively!

A couple of days later we moored around the corner nearby. I had spied a half sunken Asian wooden junk in the bay earlier that day. It was lying on the shallow sand and was still half out of the water. After dinner I put an emergency call out to the crew, 'Who wants to come and help me burn the junk?' Instantly one of the crew put his hand up to help. Gotta love the total commitment and sense of adventure!

Would you have volunteered for this mission?

The two of us set off with the required fire enhancers (paper, check; fuel, check; matches, check) and got to work. This was going to be fun. In no time at all it was on. We quickly retired back to the yacht to watch the old junk go up in flames. I have learnt the hard way not to stay at the scene of the 'crime'. Just as the fire was taking hold, it died off. The Navy was back. They must have been watching us again and had gone over and put the fire out. Damn. Job TOO well-done guys! How disappointing.

I ended up buying a yacht, going halves with my cousin Jack, Uncle Bills' son. This proved to be a great decision.

We initially used it mainly for racing off Townsville and visiting the islands between the Whitsundays and Dunk Island.

Yacht racing is a great escape from life and workplace pressures. To be competitive, yacht racing takes 100 percent concentration, hence it provides a great escape from reality. The start of a yacht race is especially demanding, and next level adrenaline if the wind is strong. Big decisions need to be made quickly, and before you are truly in possession of all the facts. This is because yachts can't turn on a dime, and judgement is required to decide if you need to give way to a competitor, or if you have time to squeeze past, without right-of-way. Getting it wrong can mean a protest, a disqualification, or worse, a very expensive collision. I worked out that the sails can provide over 120 horsepower on a windy day. This power must be controlled by ropes, pulleys, winches, experience and some luck.

In one race we got tangled up with the spinnaker ropes of a competitor's yacht. The forces were so strong it bent the stainless steel bars at the back of our yacht in an instant. I later tried to straighten out those bars with a hydraulic jack. The force required to straighten them amazed me. The wind forces had bent these in an instant.

Racing at Hamilton Island race week gives several added challenges. Many islands to dodge, strong island currents, incoming jets over the start line (I kid you not) and many more yachts to avoid. At the finish line of one race, there were so many yachts, the finish line was not long enough to fit all the boats side by side together. At 'Hammo' you get to see the big professional maxis racing close up. Wild Oats 11 and Black Jack etc. All very interesting.

Magnetic Island race week is our favourite event. It is six days of racing. It is extremely well organised and is more social than the big events to the south. The party atmosphere is more centralised and there are bands on every night where everyone gets together. If you don't have a good time at Maggie Island race week you have serious life issues. In 2024, we eventually won the Maggie Island race week series after 15 years. The celebrations were intense! Fortunately (or maybe not), videos were taken to capture the moments.

We toggled back and forth between Townsville and Brisbane four times. This is a fantastic trip, with so many deserted island opportunities along the way. Most of the scenery is just amazing, and mooring up at deserted islands each night is something else. We often do any walk that is available when on the islands. Many have national parks on them which provide great walking opportunities. The dawns and sunsets are simply spectacular. The brightness of the stars at night needs to be seen to be believed.

There are so many deserted island resorts along the way, now just ghost resorts. The owners have left behind environmental messes. Great Keppel, Brampton, South Molle, Long Island, Dunk and Lindeman Islands come to mind. Of particular note is Brampton off Mackay where we often ventured when we lived in Mackay. Also, my parents had their honeymoon there. My wife and I had our honeymoon on Lindeman.

Zen at 'full noise' during Magnetic Island Race Week.

There is a 2-day section of travel just north of Yeppoon that has no mobile phone service. We weren't aware of this on our first trip south. In addition to this Telstra did an upgrade so it meant our phones continued to not work when service resumed. It meant we were out of contact for four days, and because we didn't realise we were entering this area, we didn't warn our wives. I normally tried to let my wife know every day where we were.

By the time we got to Great Keppel Island we still didn't have reception and we knew something was not right. We were moored off the island and this boat came racing over, yelling, 'Zen, Zen the coast guard are looking for you, you're supposed to be lost'. Apparently, our wives were freaking out and rang the Yeppoon Coast Guard to report us lost. Ouch. Later my wife made me ring the Coast Guard and apologise. They were good with it and said, 'Don't worry mate, we get a lot of this'.

By the time I finally returned from that trip I had been away 5 weeks or more. We had taken our time; we had no reason to rush. I got out of the taxi and noticed a rolled-up tent on the front doorstep of our house. Unusual. As I got closer, I noticed all these signs on the door, like:

> No Vacancy.

> Hostel closed.

There was an arrow pointing to the direction of a "camping area" (the backyard!) with a tarp provided in case of rain……How thoughtful.

After some tricky negotiation with Ann, I managed to get back into the house. Maybe I had just stepped over the edge, yet again?

What do you think?

One year, on our annual sail down the coast, there were bushfires throughout Queensland and dense smoke on the water from Mackay to Gladstone. A Deep Purple song comes to mind. Visibility was only about 100 meters creating potentially dangerous situations, particularly with the LNG (liquid natural gas) cargo vessels coming into Gladstone port. This situation was more dangerous than sailing at night. At least you can see the navigation lights at night. Luckily, we had good navigation apps and managed to get through it. The eyes were stinging for a while with all the smoke; there was no avoiding it.

Another year we ventured to Hinchinbrook Island near Ingham. This is a great trip as one passes through the Palm islands and further north. We were anchored off Pelorus Island one night and two crew were sleeping in the cockpit as there wasn't enough room inside. For those not familiar with yachts the cockpit is at the back of the yacht and is open to the elements. Halfway through the night one of the crew yelled out 'man overboard' really loud. In fact, loud enough to seem serious. It was 3.00 am. Reluctantly we all stirred and rose to investigate. One of the guys sleeping in the cockpit had sleepwalked straight off the back of the yacht. He had no idea. Even in the water I don't think he had totally woken up and did not realise his situation. It was bizarre. Thank goodness the other person in the cockpit was awake at the time. We threw the guy a life ring and hauled him back in. I've never really worked out if it was funny or serious.

One night, about ten pm I was sitting on Zen and it was parked at our marina berth at the Townsville yacht club. I was doing nothing, just minding my own business. A lady walks past and heads out to the end of the marina. Next, she re-appears and goes back the other way. Then re-appears again and goes back and forth along some side fingers of the marina. She was walking slowly, in fact staggering, and was looking around everywhere. Curiosity finally got the better of me, "Everything OK, can I help you?'.

'I can't find my boat!' a slurred reply. "We got here at midday and went to the club for lunch, and I have forgotten where we parked. My husband bailed out a couple of hours ago and left me at the bar'.

Now that's a serious lunch session, from midday to ten pm! "What sort of boat is it?", I enquired thinking it would be a small boat and that's why she was having trouble finding it.

'A Bavaria 54'; more slurring.

Now that's a 54-foot motorboat, how could she not find that?

Feeling sorry I offered to help, and we eventually found it over the other side of the marina. 'Do you want to come aboard for a drink?' she asked as we got close.

Now let me think about that, 'AAHH No thanks.' Thought bubble.... Husband wakes up, hears noise on deck, comes up, sees a stranger on his boat, drinking his beer with his wife at 11.00 pm.... What could possibly go wrong?

Would you have accepted the offer???

Zen – all hands on deck

Chapter 16

The wedding and the week of honeymoon mayhem

Thirty five years and counting. I wonder what set of rapids would best represent our marriage? I am picturing a beautiful landscape, bubbling brook, lovely relaxing background murmur from the water, and rapids not so calm as to be boring but with the occasional controllable turbulence to arouse some interest. Propsting Gorge comes to mind. It is a lovely set of rapids located not too far after the Great Ravine. As the name suggests the rapids are flanked by a lovely gorge, the last of the gorges along the Franklin. The rapids are thrilling, but not dangerous. They give one a sense of adventure and exhilaration, but safely. Great, right, lock it in! Mmm, not quite.

I can't talk about the wedding without mentioning my HQ Holden. I bought it when I was at university for $600 and it never let me down. I had my Engineering mate Ed (of 12 volt blender fame) check it out, and he gave it the OK after a 3 minute assessment. It had several aftermarket additions including a power aerial, air conditioning, rubber mats under my feet to stop the water splashing up during rain, and best of all, a water injection system. Yes, you guessed right, it was Ed who installed the water injection. It allowed us to advance the timing and increase the fuel economy without the engine knocking. The other feature was that I hand-painted it every two years with a six inch brush, whether it needed it or not. I used aluminium rust preventative house paint designed for roof protection. A great and pragmatic engineering solution.

Two days before the wedding the guests started showing up, making the trip early as part of a northern adventure. Two guests turned up as I was painting the car with the trusty six-inch hand brush. 'What are you doing that for, Doug?' they asked with smirks on their faces. 'I'm just getting the wedding limousine ready', I replied. Astonished laughs all round.

The wedding went well, and we were all partying hard inside the Home Hill Greek Community Hall. Or at least I thought everyone was inside. Unbeknown to me, a group of 'friends' led by my best man (trusted engineering friend, Ed) were outside attending to the HQ (as you do). I found out later they had a crew shadowing me during the night to ensure I didn't go outside and discover what was happening!

At the end of the night, we went out to get into the car for the drive to the motel which fortunately was close by. What a sight. They had removed every door, the bonnet, and the boot, and had the regulation string of empty cans tied to the tow ball. They had cut rank with the shaving cream. Thanks guys. One of the guests was a local police officer, and his only comment was, 'You're right to drive to the motel Doug, I've got you covered'. (Fortunately I was tipped off that he had put prawn shells in the hubcaps, which explained why they were not removed!)

So, Ann and I just got in the HQ like nothing unusual had happened and drove down the main street to the motel, cans rattling loud. Oooo yeahhh!

The next day I put the HQ back together (with assistance from my new (bemused) father-in-law) and headed for Lindeman Island in the Whitsundays for part one of the honeymoon. All good, we flew there from Shute Harbour airport. We were set to fly back, but the flight was delayed because of clouds limiting visibility, it was raining hard. We finally took off in the tiny plane, with the mud splattering all over the windows as we accelerated along the dirt runway. Ann freaked out; it was fairly dramatic.

The iconic Holden HQ wedding limousine, stripped down. Thanks guys! Gotta love that hand paintwork. 1989.

Next, we were off to Cape Upstart near Ayr for part two of the honeymoon. "The Cape" needs some description for context. You can't drive there, there were no phones, only generators for power (back then) and the only accommodation was in small tin shacks. Very simple and right on the beach. It is a one-hour boat ride from the nearest boat ramp. There are about 5 sandy bays with only a few huts in each bay. In winter this place is simply fantastic, beautiful clear water and sun sets over the ocean. Fishing and swimming are the go. It is difficult not to relax. 'The Cape' stretches up from the huts, rising steeply to over 700 meters above the ocean. It is an awe-inspiring setting. (We have sailed past Cape Upstart several times and it is visible from a very long way off, due to its height.)

The partner of our good Hash friend BJ (his hash name which stands for Babinda Jail, (that's another story) owned a shack at the

Cape. We got dropped off by another friend Mullet (that's his Hash name) in his small tinny with a 25 HP outboard. Mullet was staying at his own shack a couple bays further on. We literally had the whole bay to ourselves for the next 5 days.

What could possibly go wrong?

Our only form of communication was an emergency VHF radio. Mullet's last bit of advice when dropping us off was, 'Keep the VHF on Sox, just in case I need to contact you if there's a problem'. Yeah right; Mullet was famous for his practical jokes.

The very next afternoon Mullet was on VHF, 'Sox, be ready at 5.00 am tomorrow morning I'll be round to pick you up before the waves get ugly!'.

'Yeah right, very funny Mullet, what are you talking about?'

'No, I'm serious this time Sox, there's a cyclone on the way, and we have to evacuate before the wind picks up.' An unusual seriousness in his tone finally had me convinced he wasn't on with one of his practical jokes. This was really disappointing, but there was no option. A cyclone brings with it 4-meter-high tidal surges, and these tin shacks right on the beach meant it would be perilous to stay.

Mullet was right and we evacuated early the next morning in his small tinnie, just before it was too late. The waves were starting to form from the approaching cyclone, and at times overlapped into the small tinnie. New wife, not happy! Her sense of adventure was being tested, again. Fortunately Mullet was an expert in boating and managed to get us back to the boat ramp unscathed, but saturated. We made it home in time to batten down our house at the sugar mill.

The cyclone was a direct hit on Ayr at 1.00 pm on the fourth of April 1989. Severe tropical cyclone Aivu was a category 4 to 5 cyclone with winds up to 220 kph.

We arrive back at our sugar mill house with time to prepare for the cyclone. We know the drill, everyone living in North Queensland gets well informed on what to do if there is a cyclone.

Fill water containers; check

Have canned and packet food available; check

Torch; radio with new batteries; gas cooker; check

First Aid; check

Remember - open windows on the leeward side

Our mill house is made of solid hardwood and is very well constructed. It has a verandah on two sides, and the bathroom is in the centre of the house. Authorities advise people to shelter in the bathroom, as it is considered the smallest and hence strongest room in a typical house. We are monitoring the Bureau of Meteorology (BOM) tracking map. One never knows ahead of time exactly where a cyclone will cross the coast as they can change direction. This cyclone maintains a course directly towards us. As the cyclone gets closer, my level of concern rises. Unexplainably there is also a sense of anticipation and excitement. This continues to build as one senses the changes in weather as the cyclone approaches. I have never experienced a direct hit from a cyclone, but have been on the edge of a couple. I respect the power of cyclones. It is early morning and I can feel the wind starting to pick up.

The wind is now howling. Ann and I are in the lounge room, protected by the verandah on the upwind side of the house. The intensity continues to build. The electricity fails.

Suddenly there is an almighty crash! Instantly the noise level increases. We sense that a layer of protection has gone.

Ann and I look at each other, somewhat terrified and rush to the bathroom. We grab two mattresses, one to sit on and the other to perch above us. The noise continues to increase. The crashing and banging continues.

The roof is now making really weird noises, groaning and creaking loudly. The wind intensity increases and decreases in cycles. It gets louder and louder for about three minutes then slowly reduces for another three minutes. Each time it intensifies, we just wait in anticipation for the roof to get blown off. We have never been so scared in our lives. This is something else. There is an overwhelming feeling that I am not in control of our destiny.

Eventually the eye passes over us and it is amazing how quickly the wind stops. We know this is temporary and stay inside but take a quick peek at the verandah. Broken glass and tree branches everywhere. The glass louvres are obliterated. Mango tree branches have smashed into the house. We stare in shock amazement, but have no time to soak in the scene. The wind returns so fast and we quickly retreat to the bathroom.

I got up on the roof the next day to check it. The battens holding the roofing iron on had split lengthways and were just about ready to fly off. You could easily flap the roofing iron. We went so close to losing the roof. Driving around Ayr and Home Hill the next day revealed mass destruction like nothing I'd seen before.

Roofs blown off, houses blown away, electricity poles and trees down everywhere.

It was obvious the power would be off for a long time. We decided to get out of town and find somewhere to chill out until 'normality' returned to the Burdekin.

Such was the impact of living through a cyclone, that when cyclone Yasi was initially threatening to land at Ayr in 2011, I was organising to remove my family to Mount Isa to be sure to not get involved. It ended up crossing near Cardwell, but even then, the effects were felt strongly in Townsville.

And oh yes, back at the Cape, all that was left of some of the tin huts on the beach were concrete slabs. The huts that survived had mounds of sand inside from the tidal surge (estimated at 3 metres) that occurred.

So that fairly well wraps up my honeymoon experience, and the start of a great marriage with my fantastic wife who has steered me admirably away from the edge of trouble. You could say she has managed to portage me around the worst of the rapids! (Ann comments that maybe Cyclone Aivu was a stormy start to our marriage, a sign of moments to come, and she reckons there are some similarities?!)

We have three great children (Nicola, Chris and Luke) who we are very proud of. Ann has been our moral compass, especially my moral compass. I am so lucky.

*Interestingly, at the time of final editing and publication of this memoir, Cyclone Alfred is threatening the southeast coast of Queensland – a one in 50 years event!

Chapter 17

The end of the rapids??? Brazil, September 2023

After successfully negotiating the series of rapids in the Great Ravine, there are still many challenges. Just as you are being seduced by the tranquility that epitomises the Franklin, and you think the rapids are finished, you paddle around a bend and find there are more surprises. Rapids by the names of 'The Trojan" and 'The Pig Trough' demand your undivided attention and can be a great experience.

And so describes my first years of retirement. I was enjoying a mostly retired life for about 5 years when one day my phone rang. It was an opportunity to do some consulting work that sounded too interesting to pass up. The work was cutting edge, new to the world. Sustainable aviation fuel was in its infancy, and this was an opportunity to merge this new technology with the Australian sugar industry. I was halfway to Perth in our motorhome on a three month odyssey, but the offer allowed me to work from anywhere. What the heck, why not? This work led to a study trip in Brazil 6 months later.

Brazil September 2023

Motor bikes are whizzing past us, all around, almost shaving our car. It has taken us 45 minutes to drive 3 kilometres. Our chauffeur calmly drives us through the chaos, edging our way in and out of the traffic. Time does not matter as we are having a business meeting as we go. We are in the fourth most populated city in the world, São Paulo, with 23 million people. Flying in earlier today, I have never seen so many skyscrapers, literally thousands of them, stretching for kilometres. We land in one of the four airports in Sao Paulo city.

Our government's Smart Traveller advice for Sao Paulo is," Violent crime, including mugging, armed robbery and carjacking is common."

I don't need to worry, I am in a bullet-proof car; not just pistol proof but machine gun proof which apparently is top end. The windows are 12mm thick, and it is so quiet in the car with all the reinforcements. James Bond would approve, I'm sure.

I am learning about the Brazilian cane and ethanol industry. We will transfer our learnings back in Australia to investigate making sustainable aviation fuel (SAF) from Australian sugar cane. SAF is an emerging commodity, made with an emerging technology. This is much more exciting than managing a failing sugar industry back in Australia.

I first went to Brazil in 2012 and I am amazed at the improvements since then. In Brazil the sugar mills are privately owned, and the miller also owns large proportions of the cane lands supplying the mill. The miller often owns several mills in the region. This allows for many (whole of value chain) efficiencies that do not happen in Australia. An example of this is the harvesting and transport efficiencies that we were trying to introduce into the CSR mills, as described previously (back when I was asked by the Ingham canegrowers if I knew how to get home!).

Millers in Brazil don't just make raw sugar. They also incorporate a sugar refinery and ethanol distillery into their operations. They use corn as well as sugarcane to make the ethanol and SAF. This allows for year-round production. Some mills export over 100 megawatts of electricity, a concept that has been supported by their government. They also produce pelletised fertiliser and biogas as byproducts.

Because they own the cane lands, they have more efficient control over reusing these byproducts.

The mill owners are very entrepreneurial, they make large, informed decisions quickly. They are not afraid to take risks to explore new boundaries. They are doing things successfully in Brazil that we have not even thought about doing in Australia.

The labour rate in Brazil is 15 times cheaper than in Australia. Labour rates in Australia are amongst the highest in the world, and this is a concern for our cost competitiveness, as everyone receives the same price for their sugar on the world market. There is no doubt that without our natural resources supplying the mining industry, the living quality in Australia would be very different. Ironically it is the mining industry that is the main reason for the high cost of labour in Australia. Many sugar mill workers leave for the mines every year, which adds to the complexity of managing a sugar mill. Mills need to increase labour rates to retain staff.

Because of the climate in Brazil, they can crush the cane for up to 40 weeks per year. In Australia it is restricted to 23 weeks due to rain making it impossible to crush past December.

In summary the Brazilian cane industry is very efficient compared to Australia, and it is very large, at least 30 times the size of Australia.

It is no secret that the Australian cane industry currently faces serious challenges. Twelve sugar mills have closed in Queensland in my time. Only the larger more efficient mills remain, and they are all close to not being financially sound. They cannot afford to maintain the mills properly and hence their performance is way down on what it was. This starts the spiral of lower revenues and so it goes on. My view is it is only a matter of time before the inevitable occurs.

Chapter 18

One year later, more rapids appear from nowhere

Pakistan October 2024

The traffic is mayhem. So far today I have seen the results of five different road accidents. A rolled over truck, a rolled over trike carrying a huge load of wood, and vehicles that have run into each other or into the side of the road. We are passing through a village that lines the country road for kilometres. People live close to the road in mud huts and set up their market stalls beside and very close to the road. The traffic is crazy busy. There are motor bikes, trikes, buses, trucks carrying impossibly high loads of goods, cars, donkeys pulling carts, cattle pulling carts, camels, people walking and kids playing. One truck was loaded up so high it caught the overhead electrical wires and nearly pulled them down on top of us.

It feels like we are travelling fast, but maybe it's just because there is so much traffic so close to us. I check the speed app on my phone. Nope, we are doing 80 kilometres per hour. That's way too fast in these conditions.

We are in an armed convoy travelling through countryside Pakistan. There are four cars in our convoy. In the lead is the police truck with lights flashing and siren blaring. It is a utility with four armed men in the tray. Their rifles point outwards, and they are yelling at passing traffic to get out of the way. Next car is our private security car. Then us, and the last car is another private security car. It is full of men armed with shotguns and six shooters. I feel safe despite the warnings from my government's Smart Traveller website that advised me against coming here. My wife sends me a news clip showing how seven aid workers were killed yesterday in a terrorist bomb explosion in Pakistan. She is concerned. Fortunately, I can calm her with the information that I am not near that area. Apparently I'm in a safe zone. That's good. (Late news: The day after we left Pakistan, a suicide bomber walked into a train station and blew himself up. Twenty-six innocent people died. The week after we got home, a convoy of 200 cars was ambushed by terrorists and a gun battle ensued with the armed protection guards. Fifty innocent people were killed.)

Part of my protection crew, Pakistan 2024

We are weaving in and out of the traffic, from one side of the road to the other. We are just going wherever there is a gap. We are overtaking trucks with traffic coming towards us. Remarkably the oncoming traffic seems to get out of our way just at the last second, narrowly avoiding collisions in the process. Every minute is another heart-stopping moment. I have travelled in Cairo and Sao Paulo, and it was nothing like this.

Later I bought a paper and read that there were six people killed, 1,431 people injured in 1,328 traffic accidents in the last 24 hours in the Lahore/Punjab region.

Two months earlier I received a text from a work colleague asking if I was interested in travelling to Pakistan to assist their sugar industry. Initially I was hesitant for security and health reasons and did some research to test my thinking. Before long I decided that it would be more interesting than dangerous and decided to go. Is Pakistan on your bucket list? It turned out to be a good decision. I survived, and it was an interesting trip.

Lahore Pakistan; Population 22,000,000, no subways, no commuter train network, hardly any public bus network, very few motorways and virtually no high-rise apartment living. (Apparently people don't like living in apartments.) The ultimate recipe for traffic chaos. The ultimate recipe for smog. The smog level when we were there was 880, the acceptable limit is <50. I buy the local paper and there is a full-page article on the smog, saying how nothing is being done to stop it. The paper tells me Lahore has the second highest smog reading in the world, just behind Delhi. It explains the serious impacts on susceptible people from long term exposure (or short term exposure if you have existing lung issues). It is carcinogenic because the smog particles are under 2.5 microns in size, hence they can lodge in your lungs, just like asbestos. It makes me cough when I talk, and my throat feels raspy. Apparently, traffic is 83% of the cause. I see no electric cars and there are no ethanol powered cars. The cars and motor bikes look old and spew smoke. Lahore covers 1,300 square kilometres (because there are no high-rise apartments) so you have to drive a long way to get anywhere. The visibility at midday is 300 meters, due to smog levels alone. They sometimes close the motorways due to zero visibility from smog. Then the traffic chaos goes to the next level, if that is at all possible. During my visit they closed all the primary schools for 4 days to reduce traffic and keep the children in doors. Those who can afford to, buy air purifying machines to clean the air they breathe when home.

At the airport on our departure, you could only see the next 2 planes parked at the terminal. The third plane along was lost in the smog. At 7.30 am the day was still dim, the sun extremely weak. As the plane rose through the sky, the sun 'came out' as we rose above the smog level. It was an 'enlightening' experience as I relived what real sunshine is. I had not seen proper sunlight for 11 days. It is amazing how you can get used to a dim environment and take it as situation normal.

Pakistan is an interesting place, and we learn much about it from our sugar industry hosts. There is still a strong colonial tradition remaining from when the British pulled out in 1947. The class distinction is very wide. You can see it in the incredible grandeur of the hotels and in the management in some of the sugar mills we visited. At one mill, the manager was showing me around, and he had someone to open the doors for him as he walked around, that was his job. Another person held a box of tissues out for him so he could wipe his hands if he had to touch a handrail. A third person followed us around with a first aid box, so it was there if we got hurt. A fourth person brought us water. A fifth person was his chauffeur who would drive us around the mill if it was too far to walk. There was a team of armed guards following us everywhere. Shadowing our every move. I've never seen anything like it.

The Pearl-Continental (PC), where we stayed, epitomises the colonial past. To get into the PC you first must stop for inspection before they drop the car proof barricade. This involves opening the bonnet and boot for a close inspection, a search under the car using mirrors and a sniffer dog doing its thing. If that's all good you get let inside. You then notice the eight-foot-high brick walls with the razor wire on top and the observation guard towers every 100 meters along the perimeter fence. The final part of the procedure is the body search and the x-ray machine for your luggage. You feel safe inside the PC. And you don't need to leave, it has its own shopping mall attached.

The foyer is a vast space about half an acre in area and nine storeys high. It has five massive light chandeliers hanging from the ceiling. They are about seven metres in diameter. Overall, an extreme wow factor. It is a very old hotel which was once a place for the rich British society to remain removed from reality, or was this their reality?

The PC is in stark contrast to the 40-minute drive from the airport which passes endless kilometres of ramshackle houses and shops along dirty busy streets. It is an oasis of calm and elegance in a storm of chaos and dirt.

Most restaurants and hotels don't offer alcohol for religious reasons, but it is sometimes possible to find the exception. We find a hidden sports bar at the PC and start talking to two barristers. They tell us about the legal system in Pakistan and how it still resonates from the colonial law that the British set in place. They can work easily in both Pakistan and Australia because of these leftover similarities. The PC is one of those establishments where every guest we talked to had an interesting job or interesting story to tell. It's just one of those places. We exchanged emails with the barristers as we enjoyed each other's company. At dinner later that day we get a coded message asking if we want to partake in some top shelf Pakistani snowflakes, no risk. Let me think about that, 'Aaaahhhh no thanks!'. Decisions, decisions.

I am told that when the British left, vast tracts of land were carved off to those who were well connected. This land is now worth a fortune, and this has allowed the extreme situation of the haves and the have nots to be continued.

I am told that very few people in Pakistan pay tax, and this is why the country is broke. It relies on IMF (International Monetary Fund) funding and money from countries with their own interests in mind. An example is the main highway from north to south. It has six lanes (3 each way) and there are hardly any cars on it. It was built by the Chinese to connect the ports in the south of Pakistan with China to reduce shipping costs into China. When I was there the Arab oil nations donated 3 billion dollars to help Pakistan explore for oil.

The sugar industry consulting job proves to be very interesting, and I seek out the differences between their industry and Australia. The labour rate in Australia works out to be 30 times that in Pakistan, for the same job. That's a big ratio. Amazingly, the cost of agricultural land in Pakistan is very similar to Australia. This makes leasing agricultural land very expensive and a major proportion of farming costs. Each mill has thousands of cane farmers supplying cane, most of them only controlling less than three acres. There are no supply contracts, and it is a constant negotiation for who supplies their cane to which mill, and at what cost. Competition for cane between mills is strong. The cane minimum price is set by the government and the sugar sale price is also set. It is a very difficult industry to work in for the millers. The sugar price depends only on the weight of the cane. In Australia payment is also on cane sugar content, which is important. This incentivizes the Australian grower to send in cane of decent quality, which comes at a cost.

The low cost of labour allows for very thorough maintenance at their factories. In a whole crushing season, a factory in Pakistan sometimes only has 14 hours of downtime. In Australia that number is typically 400 to 700 hours. That's a big difference. Some aspects of the Pakistan sugar industry are far in advance of Australia, some well behind. This made my tour very interesting, and I was able to assist their industry in some aspects.

During our travels we came to realise that the government was observing us very closely. It is all about keeping foreigners safe to protect them and to protect the reputation of Pakistan as a safe place to do business. The government knew where we stopped each night and at one point made contact at ten pm to ask questions because we weren't at the scheduled place. Another day some of our team had to return to the mill immediately because of some issue on the roads that they did not want us involved in. The reason was all a bit sketchy, but the directions from the government were clear, 'Go back to the mill right now and stay there until 3.00 pm.'

The utility in our convoy with the armed police inside was provided by the government and they had to be with us whenever we moved, it's government policy. We talked a bit with them, especially about cricket. When we stopped for a break one of the security guys came over and gave us an update on the cricket score, Australia vs Pakistan. We had a good chat. The utility is blazoned with their logo, 'NO FEAR'. On his shirt is another logo, 'DEATH BEFORE DEFEAT'. Gotta love that total commitment to the cause. The AK 47 is always strung over the shoulder.

I found the Pakistani people very friendly with no animosity. They are happy and enjoy life without alcohol. We played table tennis with them at their annual work-sponsored employee day out. I believe we Australians could learn some important life aspects from them.

PART THREE

Still waters run deep
The Franklin changes the nation

Lower Franklin – still waters run deep

Chapter 19

Still Waters

We finally escape the Great Ravine, and we are mighty thankful for its passing. The rainforest now comes right down to the river. Thick, impenetrable, taking over everything. So green and lush.

We enjoy the silence.

The water is flowing but slowly. The river is narrow. It must be deep. Sheer rock walls extend vertically on both sides, at times a hundred metres straight up. At the top, the trees hang out of the cliffs, balancing precariously. We stop paddling to listen to the silence. The only sounds are from distant birds. There is no wind. I lie back on the raft and close my eyes, dreaming into semi consciousness. The sun is trying to warm me up. It fails. I force myself back to reality, as real as reality can be in this wonderland.

After the great ravine, we have time to soak in the tranquillity. We pass Rock Island Bend. This provided the iconic photo that the 'no dam' protesters used to show how surreal the Franklin is. This was their anti-dam propaganda, in response to comments made by pro-dam politicians who described it as a muddy, leech infested ditch!

We are now well into the Lower Franklin stage of the river. Today we endure the last significant rapid at Big Fall and raft by Pengana Cave.

It is a large cave set in steep sheer rock cliffs with dense green forest spilling out of the rocks at the top.

We are now sitting around the campfire reflecting on our amazing adventure. We talk about how the personality of the Franklin has left a lasting impression on us. We discuss how its character has changed and how we have seen so many different aspects to it. We marvel at how we have managed to navigate this remarkable river, and at how challenging and rewarding our experience has been. It is so much work with the portaging and/or having to rope the rafts around rapids. It is the full experience, and provides us with so much food for thought.

Even though the Franklin is known for its huge sense of adventure brought on by the chaotic rapids and physically demanding portaging, there are so many other incredible facets to it. Even when the rapids are all finished the river still impresses.

Just as retirement can transition one to a calm and peaceful lifestyle, so does the lower Franklin change its character.

Majestic and unique Huon pines grace the sides of the river and hang over the edge, casting reflections in the mirror-topped waters. Polished and wonderfully carved rock galleries rise up from the waters. Limestone cliffs sometimes dominate the river's edge, inspiring the rafter to crane one's neck and look up to capture the full extent of the grandeur. These natural formations create a strong desire to just linger and soak in the ambience.

We now have a long paddle without much aid from the current. We have to reach the Gordon River, then paddle some more to get to the ferry that will take us back to Strahan on Macquarie Harbour. We have time to paddle at our own pace, to relax and enjoy the total serenity.

I look up and see two white bellied sea eagles circling above, catching the thermals. They swoop down past us, looking for food. Such magnificent birds, with wingspans over two meters. So powerful yet graceful and agile.

Chapter 20

The Franklin River springs to life and changes the nation

After the Great Ravine is the site of the proposed Franklin River dam. What an impact this dam would have had on the Franklin River if it had gone ahead. It is difficult to imagine this wonderful landscape that we had just rafted through, being totally flooded out of existence. I am so grateful for the efforts of the opponents of the proposed dam. The river won this battle and changed the political landscape of Australia forever. I ponder on the history, and its significance...

Lake Pedder was flooded by the upper Gordon River hydroelectric scheme in 1972 and the greenies were furious (the Green party was not yet really in existence, but this event was the catalyst for its formation). When the liberal-orientated Tasmanian Hydro Commission hinted at damming the Franklin River, those people who opposed the flooding of Lake Pedder sprang into action. They had had enough. There was no way they were going to let more incredible rainforests get destroyed. One of the proposals would have flooded the Franklin right back to the Lyell Highway. This meant a massive area of treasured forest and ecosystems would have been lost forever.

Support for the dam in Tasmania was very strong, because more dams meant more industry and more jobs.

Protesters in rafts took the issue to the river. This was strategically smart because the media had to show the river in the broadcasts to capture the scenes of protesters getting arrested. The natural beauty of the river had an impact on the Australian public when they saw the broadcasts. Despite this, the green movement realised they could not win their battle in Tasmania only, they had to take it federally. They targeted the marginal seats Australia-wide. Bob Hawke realised that key marginal seats were turning Green and worked out that this issue was very political and could actually assist him come to power if he

Gordon Dam

supported stopping the dam. Forward to 1983. After a long battle, the push to dam the mighty Franklin River by the Liberal federal and Tasmanian state governments was squashed. This was enabled by strong support not only from the green movement, but also from UNESCO, from the High Court of Australia and from the majority of people all over Australia. It was big news. The Greens movement gained strength from this outcome, and it was a major influence in Bob Hawkes' 1983 election victory over Malcom Frazer. This river was defining Australian history. 'Life wasn't meant to be easy' as Mr Frazer once told us. Tasmania was desperate for more electricity to power a much needed industrial and economic expansion that would deliver jobs for the unemployed. This was a very large and divisive issue. The Tasmanian Hydro Commission was very powerful at the time and had extreme support from the State government, led by Robin Gray. But taking the issue Australia-wide won the battle to save the Franklin. This issue also led to Robin Gray losing his next election (1989) with Green seats causing a hung parliament.

The influence from the Franklin did not stop there. The Greens went on to work with the Tasmanian state Labour government to double the area of protected rainforest. This protected the forests from logging, which was becoming more prevalent each year.

In 1992 the federal Greens Party, led by Bob Brown was formed. So now we have a river, so alive, that it has influenced federal politics directly and effectively. Franklin had really sprung to life. The Franklin had spread its influence right around Australia. The Greens then formed an alliance with Julia Gillard to oppose Tony Abbott. And so, the history continues.

In 2024 I re-visited Tasmania and viewed the Gordon Dam and lake area. (This is the lake that flooded Lake Pedder.) The magnitude of impact and flooding on the surrounding area is obvious. The lake extends for many kilometres on the drive in (278 square kilometres in area, 12.4 cubic kilometres in volume). The dam is huge. Tourists can walk on top of it, and it is 140 meters down to the valley below. Truly amazing in grandeur with the beauty of the river canyon directly downstream of the dam wall. This presents such a contrast in settings. The concrete dam wall and the amazing forest downstream. The construction of the dam won engineering awards when it was built. The dam construction required 154,000 cubic metres of concrete. Concrete manufacture emits large amounts of greenhouse gasses. This, along with the flooding of wonderful forests, represents a huge conundrum, as the dam has provided cheap green electricity (up to 450 MW) for 47 years and counting. There is no perfect solution for slowing global warming.

Chapter 21

The later years; the final stages of the Franklin

It is 2024 and I have returned to where we ended our rafting trip 40 years previously. This is a world heritage protected rainforest. Top shelf green environment. We are gliding along the river in an electric powered cruise boat. The memories come flooding back. The tour allows us to get off the boat and walk through the jungle. It is a magic setting of lushness. Tree trunks are covered in moss and lichens. The ground is a carpet of vegetation and fungi. Even in the middle of the summer's day it is cool and dark under the canopy. The forest spills into the river.

I learn how the forest interacts with the fungi and nutrients in the soil. I learn how pheromones are transmitted in the air when trees come under stress. I learn how trees know when another tree has reached the end of its life through the rhizomes, and then stop supporting it through this underground network to allow new trees to form. I learn how the Huon pines self clone new trees and that they can grow to be 4,000 years old. I learn about the cycle of water between trees and the atmosphere, and how rain is generated back to the forests. I learn how young growing trees need huge amounts of water, and how the river supports this need.

The captain points out a nest occupied by two white bellied sea eagles. The nest has been occupied for decades and gets reused over the generations. The two birds appear, and the deckhand throws some chicken carcasses into the water, a daily treat. The birds swoop down and effortlessly pluck the chickens out of the water. I wonder if these are the offspring to the birds I saw from the raft, decades previously.

Life goes on.

I think about the different stages of the Franklin River that I have experienced. The small bubbling shallow stream. The building of momentum as the side streams and waterfalls power in. The strong but manageable rapids that tumble over the small, rounded rocks. The uncontrollable rapids that thunder their way through the canyons in the mountains, exploding through the gaps in the giant rock formations, sending the mist rocketing high through the ravine walls. The deep slow flowing final stage that inspires deep thinking from those who pass through.

Grampians NP nerve test. My thrill seeker Mum looks relaxed with me 'risking my life'. This is living on the edge!

Now that I'm in the deep, still and mature part of the Franklin, and in the more mature deep-thinking stage of my life, it's only fitting that I provide some philosophical insights. Please allow my indulgence.

I reflect on the different stages in my life as the cruise boat slips through the final quiet stages of the Franklin. I think about how I have matured over time, even if it's better late than never. I *think of the learning experiences I've had. Of how these have changed the way I now act, react and behave. I no longer look for the more chaotic rapids in life. I am now content with calmer learning experiences. I think about me at 21 and how my values and beliefs have changed over time. I ponder what events have helped guide me on my journey and who have tamed my rapid-seeking character?*

I reflect on where the potential dams have been in my life and ponder what a new dam might look like now. I hypothesise that it is an event which would hinder me from maximising my enjoyment in life or restrict my value to society. Such an event would hold me up, or even change my life course.

I think back to my days in the Cairns courthouse. Getting verballed, changing my plea to not guilty. Three years in jail would have been a big dam.

I think about getting married and the impact this had on my character. What would have become of me if I had not married Ann? Who knows when I would have settled down. What would have become of me? The parallels between this (Ann saving me) and the people saving the Franklin are not lost on me. Interestingly I ponder about the stability of the marriages of both my parents, and Ann's parents, and that we have been married for nearly 35 years.

Mum's nerve test.
I wonder where I get it from?

I think about my decision to retire early. Staying in a toxic work environment would have created a dam in my life.

I think about what my underlying motivation in life is. A key thing for me is having to satisfy a curious mind, and to let creativity take its course. I find it interesting that these traits have not changed over time.

I think of the many correlations between the Franklin River and my journey through life.

I have a saying, 'If you're not living on the edge you are taking up too much room'. I guess the question is, 'Where is the edge?'. Is it a legal edge, or an ethical edge? Are these edges the same? Does it hurt if you step over, take the plunge? Are these edges represented by waterfalls?

I think about Maslow's hierarchical needs pyramid, and about self-actualisation. Who has achieved this? Does it matter? Where am I on his pyramid? Am I where I want to be? Where are you on his pyramid?

I think about how my sensitivity to risk has changed during my life. I realise I am now more risk averse, and consequently my life is less chaotic. I now think things through a bit more. Is that a good thing?

I wonder if, given the opportunity, would I do the Franklin again without professional guides in a one-person raft?

Which river best symbolises your life?

I have now (2024) been semi-retired for seven years. The consultancy jobs keep my mind active. I have sold my yacht and have bought a motorhome. This is a more straightforward form of travel. I can do my part time consultancy work as we travel around Australia. I enjoy a quieter lifestyle, to a certain extent. I consciously think more about, "What could possibly go wrong?", in a serious way, without flippancy.

I give back to the community. I mentor freshly graduated engineering students with their working ambitions and progress.

I take disabled people sailing. It makes their week.

Covid saw us stopping international travel and adopting more travel in Australia. We have traversed Australia from Brisbane to Perth and from Tasmania to far north Queensland in the motor home. We have discovered Australia's history along the way and seen so many beautiful locations. I had no idea Australia had so much to offer, both with the history and the beauty. I have found Australia intriguing. Tasmania is a wonderland, so many dramatic landscapes and great national parks. My advice, just do it, take your time, smell the rain forests. Take the plunge.

A day in my life in 2024

My car shows me that it is 13 degrees when I arrive at the beach. It is a ten-minute drive from home. I can see the ocean from our house, it constantly beckons me. I have a game I play; to swim at the beach every morning of the year unless the weather is crap. The life savers' black board tells me the water temperature is 21 degrees, but it looks like the chalk hasn't been renewed for a while. It is the middle of winter. I measure the water temperature by how long it takes for the pain to stop when I dive in. Last fortnight, before our cold snap, it only took about 90 seconds. Now it takes about five minutes. Ouch.

But it is worth it. It is best not to stop and think. Just keep walking into the water and start swimming when at waist level, knowing the short-term pain will pay dividends before too long. I swim flat out for 50 meters in an attempt to warm up. I fail.

Once my body is acclimatised to the chill, it is a fantastic feeling. I stop and float on my back. Blue sky everywhere, not a cloud to be seen. The sun is reflecting off the ripples on the surface. Every now and then a swell arrives and I body surf it in as it breaks on the sandbar, bubbles everywhere from the turbulence.

The beach stretches north and south. North all the way around to Noosa National Park, passing by Mount Coolum.

The water is amazingly clear. I see the fish swimming around me. Fifty metres out to sea the birds are dive bombing in an attempt to catch a meal. A soft westerly breeze is drifting by. Whales breach in the distance.

I soak in the ambience, literally. This is a great way to start the day, I know I am alive. My skin tingles.

I get out of the water and pick up my phone, it is pinging. A text arrives; Pakistan is calling.... Life goes on.

Monte Carlo – blissfully
unaware of looming trouble.

References

Anthony, Rachel, director. The Giants. Written by Lawrence Billiet, Screen Australia, 2023.

Dean, Johnson. Shooting the Franklin: Early Canoeing on Tasmania's Wild Rivers. J. and S. Dean, 2002.

Grosetti, Adam, and Kate Pappas, creators. Black Hand. Screen Australia, 2023.

The following sources were also used:

On-site signs at locations

Guided tours in Tasmania's World Heritage areas

Guided tunnel tour at Cal Neva Casino

Documentaries on JFK, Marilyn Monroe and Frank Sinatra SBS

Wikipedia sites and other internet searches

Ayr Advocate Newspaper

Appendix 1

Snapshots in time (Editor's cuts)

(Due to circumstances within my control, accuracy of dates are not guaranteed...)

i. Getting high, 2001

It's a long way down, about 10,000 feet in fact. There is no door on the one engine plane, and the air is rushing past outside. The wind noise is so loud I can hardly hear myself yelling to my instructor. I'm starting to have second thoughts but suspect it's too late to wimp out. 'Does anyone ever pull out?' I yell. 'Up here 'no' sounds like 'go' so we just jump anyway!' he replies, as he edges us closer to the place where the door used to be.

I try to relax and take in the view. Down below I can see the Townsville Strand where we will hopefully land, softly. When I signed up, they asked if I wanted to take out insurance. I replied, 'Why, if it doesn't work out, I won't need anything, just scrape me into a box!'

Wife wasn't happy with that one.

It's time to jump and there is no time to procrastinate. I am trying to remember the instructions, so we don't mess up. We're off, upside down and all I see is blue sky. I feel so out of control, so far out of my comfort zone. The adrenaline rush is like nothing else I have ever experienced. In fact, this is a total overload on my brain. We stabilise and I feel slightly more comfortable, at least I can see the ground now.

I have ordered a video as well, so another skydiver is beside us taking the shots. I wave to him and try to smile and look in control. I fail.

Before long the chute is pulled, and we are circling down gracefully. I can start to take in the serenity. Landed, high fives and big smiles all round. Happy 40th birthday, and I'm well on my way to my midlife crisis! (PS my wife insists I've had my mid life crisis, but I don't recall it ever happening!?)

ii. Shark attack, 1981

My mate Beetle and I are near Double Island point. We have only been bogged once, so that's good going. I am on my windsurfer and have just done a sail around a trawler that is parked off the beach. Sailing back to the beach I turn around to survey the view and look down behind me. Shit, a shark is following me in. It turns out a stupid idea to sail out to a trawler where they were probably sorting out their catch. Now I have to stay calm; not a good time to panic and fall in. Luckily it is a quiet day and there aren't any big waves. Steady, steady, I am almost into shore, but it is still following me, all the way to the beach. It is not a small shark either, maybe 2.5 meters long. I can see it grinning at me. I can't believe it is still tracking me, even as the front of the windsurfer hits the sand. I walk along the board and jump off onto the sand and look around. The shark now disappears out into the deep water. That's enough sailboarding for one day!

iii. Beach getaways, 1980's

We were on our way to Pottsville in my grandpas' 1900 cc Torana; five of us crammed in. We often went there to our friends' parents' beach house, or to my grandparents' place at Hastings Point. Both were good destinations for surfing and partying.

We had made it to Coolangatta and stopped for a quick beer and we each bought a carton of beer for the party. We all grabbed a tall neck (700ml) of beer for the remaining trip of about 20 minutes to Pottsville. I must have taken the corner at Kingscliff too quickly and the screech of tyres was heard by the highway patrol who soon pulled me over. Everyone, including me, tried to hide our beers somewhere, somewhat unsuccessfully. Kevin introduced himself and asked if he could have a look around. He got out his torch. All the opened beer bottles and opened cartons of beer in the boot were obvious. With the hint of a smile he asked, 'Who's been drinking in the car?'. Only one of us owned up. With his smile widening Kevin commented, 'Well you must be fuckin' thirsty mate!!'. He had a sense of humour. Good start.

I had drunk a couple of beers; no mid strength back then, and so I was close to the limit. Kevin decided to take me back to the station to do a proper test. Fortunately, this took a while to organise, and I passed the test. It was a close shave. I should have learnt from this lesson, but no.

We had a great chat during the time it took Kevin to determine if I was over the limit, and by the time he dropped me back to the car we were on first names basis. My mates picked up on this when we returned and said our goodbyes. They were impressed at my relationship building skills in times of adversity. I can't remember if they continued drinking their beers in my absence, but probably did.

iv. OUCH What the fuck was that??? 2016

Horseshoe Bay is on the Northern side of Magnetic Island, off Townsville. The best description I can think of is that the island is lost in time. This is what makes Maggie so good. It is a nice quiet getaway. Believe it or not koalas still roam down the streets at Horseshoe Bay. Because of the horseshoe shape, it is a very protected refuge for yachties. Large volcanic rocks litter the island, making it dramatically pretty. Waterfall creeks break over the rocks and trickle down to the ocean. The sun sets over the water in a magical show of colours.

We have moored at Horseshoe Bay many times.

We were swimming at Horseshoe Bay one morning and I was walking near the edge of the water. Suddenly I felt a sharp spike enter my foot. I had never felt this sensation before and intuitively knew it meant trouble. My day was about to go from penthouse to shithouse in a few seconds.

I crawled up to the beach as the pain level increased quickly and dramatically. My yachtie friends were nearby, one being a doctor. He could see the pain on my face and took my pulse. It had already doubled to 130 and he started to look a bit concerned which was unusual for him. He rang 000 and kept taking my pulse every few minutes. Someone got some ice; it made no difference. The pain was not describable. I have been surfing on my surf ski and been hit in the stomach by a nest of blue bottles. That pain was nothing compared to this. I could handle a fair amount of pain; with the blue bottles I just grabbed them, threw them to the side and kept surfing. This pain now was at the next level. It was intense and could not be budged. Removing my foot seemed like a good idea at the time. Anyone got an axe? Time passed in slow motion. I knew the medical centre was only a ten-minute drive away. Where is the paramedic? Twenty minutes went by, thirty minutes. How much longer must I wait.

Eventually, after 45 minutes the paramedic arrived. He took one look at me, gave me the green whistle (pain relief they use on the football field) and started getting a morphine needle ready. He told someone to get very hot water; apparently ice is useless on all marine stings. Soon the pain started to ease. The paramedic apologised for the delay; he was assisting someone with a bad hangover. Sometimes I find it difficult to find the right words to describe my feelings, especially without swearing!

I still don't know what I stood on, probably a stone fish. Being winter I doubt it was a jellyfish.

v. Hello, is the Queen available? 2000

We had just had a long weekend, had the Monday off, and we had packed a fair bit into the extra day. I was sitting around with the family and a couple of Hash friends, and we were trying to work out the reason for the day off. Someone piped up that it was the Queen's birthday (Queen Elizabeth II, that is). We had had such a good day out, there was only one obvious thing to do.

I rang operator assistance and found out the phone number for Buckingham Palace, along with all the country and area codes that were required back then. No mobiles.

Because it was late enough at night, the time in London was reasonable; perfect, let's do this.

The phone starts ringing and I'm thinking, wow this is actually working. Someone picks up, 'Hello this is the palace'.

'Hi there, I am ringing from Australia, can I please speak to the Queen', I replied.

A very short sharp reply, 'Sorry, not available'.

I try again, 'Sorry you don't understand, we have just had a great day off work, and it's because Lizzie gave us the day off for her birthday. I just wanted to say thanks from the convicts! We didn't have to break any rocks today.'

Click. They hung up and that was that. No sense of humour those Poms!

vi. Anyone for chocolate crackle cake? 2000

I have had numerous (friendly) encounters with police at house parties, but the night of the chocolate crackles takes the cake!

We were preparing for BJ's birthday party the following night. A few of us had gathered at Wrinkles' place to make a cake for BJ. The only cake we had any idea on was the chocolate crackle recipe on the back of Wrinkles' rice bubbles box. Perfect. This was going to take a while, so we checked Wrinkles' fridge for drinks and turned up the music. Grease saved the day when she drove in from Mackay and just happened to have a sifter in her car boot!

Just as we were finishing up the police turned up at the front door.

'We have had a complaint about the noise, you'll have to turn it off', they volunteered.

'That's no problem', I responded, 'but this is not the real party, we're just preparing the cake. The proper party is tomorrow night when BJ gets here, you'll have to come back for that as well'. I could see from the expressions there was no sense of humour. Never mind.

The next night we bring out the prized cake at the appropriate time. BJ was very impressed, no hash birthday had ever been blessed with a cake, this was groundbreaking. BJ goes to cut the cake, but it was so hard there is no way the cake is going to get cut with a knife.

Cutting chocolate crackle cake for my 40th Birthday Party in 2000 – note the responsible use of PPE.

Without blinking, BJ finds an axe and says, 'No problem, we'll sort this out!'.

Down comes the axe and splints the chocolate crackle cake into pieces. Job done.

I was so impressed with the event that on my next birthday I ordered a chocolate crackle cake and staged a re-enactment. It went well. I took all the precautions as I was now a manager and had to lead the safety awareness. I donned safety boots, safety glasses and hard hat. My father-in-law took six steps back, looking bemused, once again.

vii. Mount Garnet adventures: the wild west experience, 1988

There is a great camping trip from Ingham to Kennedy to Blencoe Falls (camp next to Herbert River) to Undara Lava Tubes to Mt Garnet then on through to Port Douglas. We took the tourist route, which means going through cattle properties, and following very detailed maps to avoid getting lost. It takes in a mixture of grazing land, rivers, hills and interesting geological features. It is a great landscape. My wife and I did this trip many years ago and had some interesting times along the way. It takes about five or six days if you take your time.

I was filling up the legendary HQ Holden at Mt Garnet and popped the bonnet for the precautionary check. (Mt Garnet is a small town 100 km to the southwest of Cairns, as the crow flies. It is much further by road.) With the bonnet up I noticed a small drip, drip of oil onto the concrete. A closer inspection revealed that the sump plate had been pierced. It was only a small leak, but it needed to be fixed as we had many lonely miles to go.

I put the bonnet down and declared to Ann, 'I think we'll stay here the night". I then realised it was late Saturday afternoon. A thought crossed my mind, 'Maybe we'll stay the weekend?'.

We found a small motel to stay in, without too much effort. We patted the old horse nearby that was tethered by a rope to the tree outside our room. Nice touch. The problem was finding a mechanic late on Saturday. I found the number for the RACQ. With much detective work (no mobile phones) I eventually managed to track down the owner of the RACQ garage. He was at the local pub, big surprise, not.

By the time I found him, the pub party was in full swing. Obviously, no repairs were happening that day. He gave me his home address and we arranged a time to meet him the next morning.

I left Ann at the motel and found his house ok. He was dressed up ready to work. Thongs, shorts and a singlet. Yes, a good start, hmm. He had a car hoist at his home garage and raised the HQ up about six feet off the ground. He then drained what was left of the oil out of the sump and started to set up to braise over the hole in-situ. Flabbergasted, I stepped up and said, 'Aren't you going to remove the sump plate to repair it?'. 'Nah mate, I do this all the time, no worries!'. So here he is, about to light up an engine full of flammable leftover liquids and gasses. Interesting. I stepped back about ten big paces and watched with a healthy mixture of interest and concern. "BOOM" The engine exploded, and a perfect cone of bright blue flame stretched from the sump plug opening right down to the ground where it burnt the tops of his feet. He sprinted to the nearest hose and started washing his feet as he swore. 'Good thing you had your safety boots on', was the only comment I could muster.

'Ah, I think I'll take the sump plate off', he volunteered when his feet had cooled down. The rest of the repair job was less eventful, and I ventured back to the motel.

First thing I noticed was no horse. Strange. I also noticed the rope that had tied the horse to the tree was still there, but it went from the tree into our motel room. Very strange. The motel room door was open. This town was becoming quite intriguing. I investigated the motel room to see the horse standing in the middle of it with Ann, trapped, further along on the far side of the room. The horse was staring at Ann. 'Hello, everything OK?' I asked, trying not to smile too much. All Ann could say was, 'I opened the door, and the horse was standing right there in front of me. I stood to the side, and it walked straight past me and came in!'

'Ah-hah, I think it's time we get the hell outta this place', I replied then gave her a summary of what had happened to me.

Fortunately, the repair job lasted until we finished our outback odyssey.

viii. Cooktown re-enactment ceremony police encounter, 1987

It was a big trip, a bunch of Hash House Harriers travelling to Cooktown for a look around and to take in the annual reenactment of James' landing at the Endeavour River.

It was a big showing, lots of people had turned up and the first nations people were huddled around their fire nearby, getting ready for 'trouble'. An area beside the river had been roped off, I guessed this is where the boats were going to come in. The crowd was all lined up behind the rope waiting for the boats to turn up.

Then when James' long boats are about 50 meters offshore, one of the harriers says to me, 'Sox there's a bottle of Malibu in it for you if you jump that rope and swim out to the boats, right now.' It was one of those compelling offers, a moment in time. There was no way it could be turned down. Would you have taken the plunge?

So off with the shirt and I had a swim. Coming back to shore a policeman strolls over to me. He is obviously having trouble controlling the smirk on his face. 'You're not doing that again are you?' he says.

'All good, job done', I say as I stroll past, not waiting to see if it's going to get complicated.

ix. Petrie Terrace watch house, 1979 (now called The Barracks)

Near the intersection of Milton Road and Petrie Terrace (Brisbane) there used to be a fast-food shop. It was very popular with party revellers because it never shut. You could always rely on it to be open for some greasy food after a big night out. I frequented it often.

I was there one night with two friends, and we'd finished eating. I forget who but one of us suggested, 'Let's go for a ride on the bonnet of the car'. Sounded like a good idea at the time, what could possibly go wrong?

We didn't realise there was a cop station right across the road, that's what. In hindsight the cops must have been laughing. We were only going slow and yes two cops pulled us over. We end up inside the watch house for questioning. One of us was a trainee lawyer, and he had all these fancy pens in his pocket. We had to hand over all our possessions as we got checked in. Apparently that's the protocol when you're staying a while.

'They're nice pens', the cop says as my friend hands them over. My friend replies, 'So long as I get them back when we leave, I'll be happy!'. Oh no, not good, I guess he needs to sharpen his negotiating skills. The copper goes into a big tirade about how they can do whatever they want, and if you continue to be smart, we'll take you out the back and show you how we really do business around here; bla, bla, bla. Time for damage control. Time to be nice. Eventually we were released with a token bail.

x. Two train events, England 1990, Canada 2017

My wife and I are on British rail heading down to Cornwall. She has just gone to the toilet and I'm sitting back reading the travel book on what to do in Cornwall.

All of a sudden, the train screeches to a halt. My wife is returning from the toilet with a weird expression on her face. I am quickly joining the dots. "Oh no, you didn't, did you?".

Oh yes, she did. Before long the conductor appears, 'Who pulled the chain, who pulled the chain?' he is yelling. My wife steps up, 'I thought I was flushing the toilet, sorry'.

The conductor just rolls his eyes and walks off, no 50 pound fine thank goodness.

We are on the Canadian Mountaineer train trip. Very nice, very expensive. Glass windows everywhere showing the most amazing views. Everyone is drinking Baileys Irish Cream like there is no tomorrow. It's 11.00 am. When we first stepped into the train we received our official briefing. 'Now you might hear some noises from the windows, a sort of crackling sound. There is absolutely no reason to worry, it's just the windows moving a bit as we go along. The windows are very strong, over half an inch thick, bullet proof in fact. They will never break'.

Later that day, C-R-A-C-K what the hell was that!? One of our travel companions has a look of horror on her face! My wife has the window seat, and I look across to her. The window has a spider web of cracks all through it. Holy crap! That's not supposed to happen, apparently. The lady who gave us the initial briefing is walking past serving Irish Cream. She is busy. 'Excuse me,' I get her attention, 'you may want to take a look at that window'.

'Oohhh' she replies, 'I've never seen that before! I'll get the conductor.'

Soon the conductor turns up and takes one look. 'Oohhh, I better get the train engineer' and takes off.

Soon the train engineer turns up. 'Oohhh, I better get the train general manager.'

Before long the train general manager turns up. So, we get to meet the complete hierarchy. We are moved away from the window and the general manager apologises. We say, no problems and tell him we still think the train is a great trip. I just love his reply, 'Don't fall asleep, because it will be the most expensive sleep you ever have!'.

It turns out that a tree had fallen over next to the track, and it had smashed into our window. What are the chances of that? Very lucky the windows are so strong, or there could have been glass smashed everywhere.

xi. Venice 1984

Venice was a highlight; the annual carnival was in full swing. I mixed with the locals and ended up at a party in a Venetian mansion. Venice is such a different place; I would say unique. It is about a one hour walk from the train station to the main centre. The walk involves meandering along the twisting footpaths beside the canals. There is no need for a guide map. Just follow the crowds. You cannot get lost. There are no vehicles in Venice, just pathways. It is a shame it is now so overcrowded with tourists. Same goes for Hong Kong.

The Venetian casino in Las Vegas has recreated life in Venice. The top level of the casino has recreated a setting straight out of Venice with footpaths, canals, gondola rides, cafes, and Italian red wines. It must cover a hectare in area with a very high domed ceiling. The artificial sky creates a 24/7 sunny day with clouds moving across the ceiling. It is an amazing artificial re-creation like nothing I have seen anywhere else.

xii. Welcome to East Germany - one year after the wall comes down, 2000

We are on the autobahn, doing 170 kph. I feel safe, it is a long straight ride and Christian seems in control. I look behind and see a car about a kilometre back. It is flashing its lights furiously. It is approaching us so quickly; I recheck our speed because I don't understand. In no time at all the BMW limo flashes past us. It must be sitting at 240 kph. Now that's what I call life in the fast lane!

We have been staying with Christian and his family in Wuppertal, West Germany. He has been showing us all around his region, and it's been very interesting. Lots of industry (think Krupp and Bayer) and beautiful locations. I know Christian because I met his sister Helga in Japan when on my world trip. Helga and Christian subsequently came and stayed with me in Ayr. I introduced them to Hash House Harriers, it was a memorable cultural immersion for them.

We are now on our way to East Germany. The wall has been down for one year, but there is still border security. We approach the border guard and stop, roll the window down. 'That will be 40 Deutsche marks each for the visa please', he says. I know the value of a west Deutsche mark is four times the eastern version so I ask, 'Will that be eastern or western Deutsche marks?'. 'That will be Western if you don't mind, we have enough eastern. Danke Schön!'.

We are staying with Christian's friends. It is a really interesting insight into life in a communist country. The family was quite wealthy at one time, but that ended quickly when the war started. They owned a business but it was resumed by the government. They now survive but life is very plain, no frills. We have brought with us some western luxuries and shared them around. They are very grateful.

xiii. 28 hours in Santiago Airport, 2023

Before I left home, I checked my itinerary quickly, and ascertained I had a four-hour stopover in Santiago on the way home. No need for a Chilean visa then. It would just be a quick transfer.

We were going to Brazil for 8 days on a consulting trip to investigate their cane and ethanol technology. Halfway through the week I was talking to my work colleagues about their return flights when it dawned on me my layover was actually one day and 4 hours. That's what can happen when you read an itinerary quickly, and the travel agent doesn't give you the heads up.

Anyway, no harm done, I applied for an e-visa and just before I left Brazil I received an email in Spanish. Google translator was a bit ambiguous, but I think it said the visa was "successfully received". I assumed I was good to go, but a little warning in my head said it may not all be sweet.

My chauffeur takes me to the airport, and I ask him to park and come in with me, not just drop me off. I know that if my travel documents aren't right, the check-in people won't let me on the plane. If this happens, I'll ask the chauffeur to take me to the hotel while I sort things out.

After some checking with the area manager of the airline departures counter, I am given the OK. As a precaution I book my bags through to Australia, even though I have a hotel booking in Santiago for a night. I pack a change of clothes in my carry on. I still am not sure all will go well in Chile, and I don't want my bags offloaded in Santiago if I can't get to them.

I am in Santiago and get waved up to the border security guy. He is looking at my passport. He says "visa" and I show him the email on my phone with a hopeful smile. He reads it and starts phoning people. Several people. I have been waiting patiently, then he says," Stand over there, visa not ready". I wait for several more minutes. Eventually another customs person turns up, a Chilean lady packing a six shooter on her belt. 'Follow me' is all she says, no time to be nice. She takes me through into the backrooms of the customs area, 'Sit down over there'.

I wait for another ten minutes which gives me time to think.

Best case, I get to my hotel for the night.

Worst case, I get to spend some time in a Chilean jail.

In between scenarios, I spend 28 hours at the airport or I am sent back to Brazil.

After what seems like a long time, a man comes over and starts asking me all these questions about how I applied for the visa, what app I used etc. etc. I eventually work out they must be having issues with fake visa web sites and want to check if I used one of them.

Another ten minutes of sitting around, and I am taken into another room. Finally, the official says, 'Your only option is to stay at the airport overnight. You are not allowed into Chile.'

'OK I'm fine with that.' I reflect on the good call I made to put my luggage through to Australia, not Santiago.

167

I get shown the door back out to the upstream side of customs. I find my way to the Latam Airways lounge. Fortunately, my flight ticket allows me access. I have been in some nice business lounges in my time, but the Latam airways lounge at Santiago takes the prize. It is their signature lounge, and I have fallen on my feet. I have 28 hours to fill in. I sleep for the first 13 hours in a private bedroom. Everything is available, 24-hour cocktails, nice Chilean food and red wines, freshly squeezed orange juice etc. etc. There are workstations, cinema rooms and child-minding rooms. I do some work, take it easy, and go for a long walk in the airside of the airport. I think back on the movie where some guy spent weeks in an airport. I write some more of my memoir.

It's time to board my next flight.

If you ever fly to Santigo, make sure you get a window seat. The plane flies along beside the Andes Mountain range for like an hour, and the scenery is amazing.

Somewhat relieved, I find my luggage when I arrived back in Australia.

xiv. A day in the life of a sugar mill production manager

A sugar mill is a very challenging and interesting place to manage. Cane comes in with very varied quality characteristics, eg: various dirt levels, grass levels, sugar content; it can be dead or stale; it can contain steel or logs. From this, it is turned into crystal sugar which has ten strict quality requirements, from moisture content, colour, temperature, sucrose (sugar) content, grain size and others not visible to the naked eye.

There are several steps in making sugar: crushing the cane, clarifying the juice, crystalising the juice, separating the crystals and cooling and drying the sugar to name a few. There is a huge focus on not losing sugar in the process. This can happen physically, by sugar literally being washed down a drain, or with chemical reactions in which sugar turns into gasses which are not visible. Sugar can also be retained in the byproducts eg molasses, fibre or mud. A 1% loss of sugar in the cane can cost over $1,000,000 per year to an average mill.

A production manager needs to work well with other managers, maintenance engineers, operators, cane growers, unions and government authorities for environment compliance and safety compliance.

The factory operates 24/7 from June to December. The manager is always on call to assist when there are problems. When a factory stops, time is ticking at over $8,000 per hour. The pressure is on.

A typical day may involve:

- analysing the issues from overnight reports,
- walk the factory to touch base with overnight operators,
- lead morning production meeting to organise how to solve operational problems,
- write reports,
- attend any other meetings; capital, safety, environment, industrial, growers etc.
- attend to other operational issues that crop up during the day.
- Show visitors and/or upper management around the factory.
- Sort out any disciplinary or union issues.
- Manage staff development and succession planning.
- Write more reports.

From December to June the factory is pulled apart and maintenance is completed. Capital construction is also undertaken, and the capital required for the next 3 years is planned. Production managers get involved in everything for advice.

The day is very busy, and time passes so quickly. There are literally no idle moments. I have heard many retired managers comment that they didn't realise how intense their job was until they left.

Management requires a delicate balance of being firm and strong with employees, but keeping the workforce motivated.

I never stopped learning in over 36 years of working in the sugar industry.

xv. Enjoying retirement???

When I announced my early retirement, one of my university mates casually said to me, 'Early retirement is not straight forward'. This comment proved to be more insightful than I first realised. Many of my work colleagues of similar age are still working. I am often asked about retirement when I reconnect with them. Not just a rhetorical question in passing to make conversation, but a very intentional question seeking information. They are deeply considering retirement but are procrastinating as they weigh up all the pros and cons. I think maybe some of them are sort of afraid, or maybe at least hesitant to take the leap.

When asked, my answer to the retirement dilemma is not quick and simple. There are a lot of hours in each day. Simply sitting around all day is not good. One needs to have many different options to remain active both physically and mentally.

I recommend part retirement as a first step. I continue to consult on the more interesting offers that come my way. This also gives me a sense of satisfaction as I am contributing to successful outcomes.

One of the basic needs for people is to feel wanted. To this end I give back to the community through things I also enjoy doing. An example of this is sailability, where I take disabled people for sailing boat rides. Sailability is an Australian wide organisation and is very well run.

Exercise (both physical and mental) is also so important. I walk for over one hour most mornings, then swim in the ocean. Social interaction is also important. I am a member of several groups where this happens.

The other aspect is where you retire. Our house and yard require a reasonable level of maintenance. This is good as we can get satisfaction from improving our house and gardens. Gardening can be therapeutic. We are also happy with our location on the Sunshine Coast. The climate is great year-round, and we don't need to use air conditioning. We get a good ocean breeze living on the side of a hill.

In summary:

Keep mentally and physically active

Pick the right time but don't procrastinate about this

Pick the right place

Transition with part time work

Do things which give you a sense of accomplishment

Create social networks in your life

Have fun

Appendix 2

Notes from Burdekin Hash House Harriers circa 1980's

Everyone in Hash House Harriers Club gets a nickname which signifies a significant event, a stuff up or a play on words to do with their name or profession. It's best not to ask the reasons behind a hash name as this may prove embarrassing! All in good fun and members (well, most) were happy to go along with it. A few of the names may seem offensive – but in the 1980's we were unaware of these sensitivities.

My memory has failed me so apologies to those who I have omitted.

Some names in Burdekin Hash were:

Gutterbuster	Wrinkles
Nipple	Tartus
Animole	Boomer
Bogman	Groper
Pecker	Hot Dot
Barnacle / Mrs Smith	Pokey / Mrs Backbar
Sneeze / Flusher	Killer
Rowdy	Blackie
Phantom	Sludger
Grease	Longjohn
Rotary-hoe	Stitch
Jerkit / BJ (Babinda Jail)	Tripod

Mullet	FIM (foot in mouth)
Halfa	Double D

Each week Hash notes were published in the local paper. Some people thought they were interesting, to the point of purchasing the local paper solely to read the hash notes. Enjoy.

The Ayr Advocate Newspaper: Hash House Harriers Column

BLACKIE MAKES HASH HISTORY

6/3/1987

History was made last week when Blackie led the field for most of the run.

He ground to a halt however with 8 furlongs to go when Mrs Smith came up from the rear to take the lead along with Jerkit who finally won the race. Blackie was showing good form until he ran out of air and came to a spluttering stop.

The run went for 4.5 kilometres through very rough and wild-west type country. The Hash spirit, unhindered by wild bulls and barbed wire, once again raged on.

It was a pleasant On On, on the veranda of Rotary's mansion with a top Hash nosh stew served up by BJ and his harem. BJ has never failed us with his tin nights.

Normally the word 'tin' falls into the category of alcohol for a Hash man and many were surprised at the viscosity of the contents of the tins and they were ceremoniously opened.

Which brings me to the topic of "Super-Novas and the meaning of life".

Did you know that it took exactly 42 super-nova explosions to form the universe hence creating a 'user-friendly' environment. No more, no less and that's why there is intergalactical resistance against a nuclear war. You see, any more supernova-type influences will destabilise the milky way with consequential effect on this and neighbouring universes.

Hash people around the world know this hence the reason for international gatherings with an "everyone's a winner" philosophy. Hash people don't drink because they are insecure or are starved of attention. They simply enjoy non-competitive, greedless and mellow environments wherever they venture.

See for yourself this Monday at the Delta at 6 pm. A barbeque will follow, and the Delta pool should serve to drown any conspicuous comments.

On On

Animole

GROWING CONFIDENCE IN HASH

13/3/1987

Good attendance and a dedicated effort, a reflection of the rising characteristics of last Monday's run.

Some new runners were also present, and we made sure that they got clued in on the intricacies of Hash.

Hash is particularly popular at the moment with the cool weather making conditions very attractive for a quick 5-mile sprint around Ayr's suburbs.

Phantom Two, general manager and spokeshashperson for the Burdekin group stated that a contributing externality to hash enthusiasm was created by growing interest arising from Hash's extracurricular activities such as basketball, golf, indoor cricket, night soccer and Almost Anything Goes competitions.

In a report tabled in hash parliament last week, where incidentally personality warfare and derogatory comments are banned because the nature of the tabled reports is of a very serious matter which does not seem to be apparent in other houses of parliament. Phantom Two indicated that his bidependence should be offset on the horizontal axis by a community involvement factor.

In other news this week, Belinda was welcomed to the Hash organisation and Gutter Buster had his 5oth anniversary – the quickest on the record books. We also welcomed a lost runner, Grease who has been lost for two years but has slipped back into the grips of unreality. Remember reality is for those who can't handle hash.

Next week's run starts from the Kalamia Hotel at 6.oopm. Barbecue will be hot.

On On

Animole

HASH HOUSE HARRIERS

Date unknown

Last Monday saw the successful completion of what is commonly referred to as a city sprint.

This is a short run through the inner city with many hold checks – normally at places of interest. It is a recognised fact that these runs also stimulate the town's economy and that they normally occur when Blackie sets a run – funny about that.

The last but not least place of interest raised at the On On were the results of a recent survey conducted by a group of interhash post-doctorate psychologists who have spent their last 5oo hash runs studying the subconscious attitudes of runners in their respective groups from around the world.

They have managed to correlate the distance that a runner stays away from a gutter when he runs along the footpath to his subconscious level of self-actualisation.

"So what?" you may well ask.

They plan to extrapolate their results in the areas of career marketing by subjecting applicants to varying hash runs as part of a new concept in interviewing techniques.

The money raised will go towards bettering the hash facilities at annual interhash meetings and into further research by stating that this was just another example of how hash is constructively interacting with today's society.

Next week the findings will be applied in Home Hill at 6.00pm starting in First Street outside the Home Hill High School. A meal will be served to those whom it is considered have appropriate self-esteem.

On On

Animole

HASH MEN GET LOST!

22/2/1987

BJ set a confusing and frustrating run last week which had the desired effect of splitting the pack up so that the fast runners didn't finish too far ahead.

The ideal run has runners of all standards finishing together. This happens because the faster runners run off further seeking out the false trails.

This has a strong analogy to a person's real income. It doesn't matter how much money you earn gross, you still net about the same amount. Another analogy is the international export potential of a country. You see, this is really independent of the country's economy because the export potential is balanced by the strength of that country's currency.

An economically strong country might be able to produce goods cheaply for their domestic market but they will be beaten by exchange rates on the international scene. Hence real international significance can only really be tested at inter-hash meetings where thousands of competitions from over 500 countries get together to decide which is the strongest country.

It is from the results of these annual meetings that politicians should determine a country's strength and hence their export potential for this is the only externality-free method in gauging these values.

In other significant events this year, the Bogman got a hash naming and Rotary-Hoe got a down down for turning up late – again. He is the most consistent non-runner we have.

Next week's run is from opposite the Max Motel near the showgrounds at 6 pm instead of a barbecue we're having a can night so bring an edible can along. No pet food please.

On On   Animole

HASH HOUSE

19/6/1986

Fozzie went out of his way to make a nuisance of himself last Monday by setting a long run with long false trails.

There is no excuse for this sort of behaviour hence the bear was punished with a down, down.

The other big news for the week was that Wrinkles had a double down. Not only did he celebrate his "real life" birthday but also his Hash centenary. He was aptly rewarded.

Wrinkles is one of the few founding runners of hash in the Burdekin and we all had quite an interesting night sitting around the campfire, listening attentively to the old master recalling the bygone days. "I remember the days" he would recall, "when your average false trail was 1.5 miles long and if you didn't do it you got ten lashes by the mother superior!"

Yes, you could still see the twinkle in his eyes as he adjusted the burning embers with his walking stick and pulled the collar of his dressing gown more tightly around the sagging skin of his neck.

"Those were the days" he would continue, his voice shaky yet firm, "when instead of a hash horn, we had a hash whip, and it was no place for short-cutting wimps!"

Anyway, enough of the history lesson. We should just be thankful for the way things are at present and endeavour to provide future generations with a suitable springboard from which they can jump into a healthy existence.

Basic extrapolation of points defining the criteria for the meaning of life indicate this goal will be realised by a self-governing philosophy, not to mention the availability of genetic engineering.

See you at the Ayr Bowling Club next Monday at 5.30pm. Barbecue to follow the exercise.

On On

Animole

Sockhill family: Luke, Ann, Me, Nicola and Chris at K'gari 2024.

Acknowledgements

A sincere thank you to my writing tutor, Pauline du Rietz for her guidance and encouragement; friends Nerida, Antoinette and Peter for their feedback and support; Belinda Walker and Melanie Brasch (Just Sparkle Books) for the valuable advice and assistance with publishing.

Our children, having heard some of the stories, suggested I jot them all down as they are recalled and collate them. They have been a source of encouragement along the way.

Nicola, Chris and Luke, we've steered through mostly fun rapids together. Let's continue to enjoy the ride! We are so proud of you all.

I would like to thank Angela, Rob and my other rafting colleagues for their invitation to raft the Franklin and for providing the action photos for this book. Those of you who captured those moments did a magnificent job in such a challenging environment.

To you the reader, thanks for picking this book up and making it to the end! We have all had our challenges, whether chosen or not. I hope this book helps you to reflect on the positive ones and inspire you to seek out new adventures.

This is a true story. Some of the names have been changed to protect the innocent from potential legal proceedings or embarrassment.

www.ingramcontent.com/pod-product-compliance
Lightning Source LLC
Chambersburg PA
CBHW042047290426
44109CB00006B/133